Shadow Banking and the Rise of Capitalism in China

Andrew Collier

Shadow Banking and the Rise of Capitalism in China

Andrew Collier
Orient Capital Research
Hong Kong

ISBN 978-981-10-2995-0   ISBN 978-981-10-2996-7   (eBook)
DOI 10.1007/978-981-10-2996-7

Library of Congress Control Number: 2017934895

Cover illustration: © WorldFoto / Alamy Stock Photo

Printed on acid-free paper

This Palgrave Macmillan imprint is published by Springer Nature
The registered company is Springer Nature Singapore Pte Ltd.
The registered company address is: 152 Beach Road, #21-01/04 Gateway East, Singapore 189721, Singapore

"I would like to dedicate this book to my long-suffering assistant, Shiyi Zhou, a very smart and talented analyst from Shanghai. She has ably pulled together data—from official and unofficial sources—and combined this with penetrating analysis of how the Chinese economy really works. This book would be much the poorer without her excellent assistance."

Contents

LIST OF FIGURES

CHAPTER 1

Introduction: The Mayor of Coal Town

THE MAYOR OF COAL TOWN

In 2006, Xing Libin was a small-town coal entrepreneur in the hardscrabble town of Liulin in Shanxi province. Liulin (pronounced "lowlin") is one of China's poorest towns, where the air is thick with coal dust and the run-down buildings look more like a movie set of a ragtag Western than the heartland of China's booming industry. But running through the soil of Liulin and its nearby towns in Shanxi like diamonds on a necklace were thick veins of coal. And that was the source of Xing Libin's rise. The 47-year-old lawyer was schooled at the local Shanxi University and made his first money in the 1990s renting a coal mine in the small town of Liulin (population 320,000) from the county government. Through a series of astute investments, along with good political connections, Xing amassed a collection of coal mines and transformed them into a company that came to dominate a large chunk of the coal fields of Shanxi province, which churns out one-third of all the coal in China. In 2011, Forbes magazine called him one of China's 400 richest businessmen. His power extended to the political realm. Locals viewed him as the unofficial mayor of the town. At one point, he owned the hotel, the largest office building, the largest residential complex, and built his own school. If you wanted to get something done, Xing Libin was your man.

As with many of the ultrarich in China, Xing liked to flaunt his wealth. When his daughter Jing was married in May of 2012, Xing Libin hosted

© The Author(s) 2017
A. Collier, *Shadow Banking and the Rise of Capitalism in China*,
DOI 10.1007/978-981-10-2996-7_1

1

an $11 million wedding featuring a ceremonial coach and horses driven by foreign coachmen. He flew hundreds of people on privately chartered planes to an expensive resort on the tropical island of Hainan in Southern China, thousands of miles from cold and dusty Shanxi province, for the gala wedding. For the dowry, he gave his new son-in-law six red and white Ferrari cars. His daughter posted pictures online, flaunting her status as a rich, new wife. It was a glorious moment for a man revered by locals as the kingpin of their town.

But the fortunes of Xing Libin changed very radically. Two years later, Xing Libin's position at the top of the rich in China came to an end. His company collapsed, leaving debts upward of $3 billion. And the empire he built in the small town of Liulin in Shanxi was gone.

As I looked into Xing Libin and his various companies, I realized the story of Xing Libin is the story of Shadow Banking. Xing had built his empire on Shadow Banking loans. When his firm collapsed, he defaulted on 15.3 billion renminbi in bank loans and 7.3 billion in loans from a type of a Shadow Bank called a Trust. These Trusts had been around for a while as bit players in the world of finance. In fact, Shadow Banks had existed in one form or another since the beginning of China's reforms in the 1980s under Premier Deng Xiaoping. But they exploded in 2008, following China's panic-driven stimulus package. That was when Beijing rammed 4 trillion renminbi (US$600 billion) down the throat of the Chinese economy in an ultimately successful attempt to keep China from being dragged through the mud of what turned into a global financial crisis. A flood of money poured through China's economy outside of the officially sanctioned state-owned banks. Instead of nice, orderly bank loans, the money flowed through a new group of "Shadow Banks" that sprang up like weeds.

As one of the premier scholars of China's informal finance, Kellee Tsai, noted: "The 2008 stimulus incentivized various state actors to participate in shadow banking: local governments, state banks, and SOEs" (Tsai 2016).

Shadow Banking is one of those terms that refers to anything from drug barons sending money by telegram across the globe to mortgage derivatives that contributed to the 2008 American Great Financial Crisis. At root, the term Shadow Banking really is just a catch-all label for non-bank lending. Modern Shadow Banking originated in the USA in the early 1970s in the form of money market funds that served as an alternative to bank deposits when deposit rates in the USA were still controlled by the Federal Reserve (Bottelier 2015). In China, though, Shadow Banks have a particular meaning and relevance to the Chinese economy. Two of the main scholars on Shadow Banking in China, Jianjun Li of the Central University of Finance and Economics in Beijing, and Sara Hsu of the State University of New York at New Paltz, note that money collection in China comes in three forms: approved by the central bank, cleared by the local government, or not authorized by anyone. Shadow Banking falls into the third basket.

When Mao established the People's Republic of China in 1949, he put in place a rigid state apparatus to control political, economic, and even cultural life. On the economic front, virtually all activity was funneled through a small group of state institutions. These included local institutions such as farming cooperatives, where everyone shared the workload and was guaranteed a minimum standard of living, to giant steel mills, employing hundreds of thousands of workers. No one was allowed to buy or sell anything outside of this state system. This vast web of economic actors was in theory controlled by the State Planning Board in Beijing through a system of "inputs," like coal and iron, and "outputs," like steel. The money for everyone in the system came from the central bank in Beijing. When I was a graduate student at Yale reading up on the early years of the People's Republic of China, we would joke that we doubted there was a blackboard large enough to handle all the many different inputs and outputs an economy as large as China would require. Not only was this cumbersome to manage—the bureaucrats would certainly need a ton of chalk—but it also was inadequate to the task of allocating resources to an increasingly complex economy.

This rigidly controlled economy changed radically shortly after the death of Mao in 1976. When Deng Xiaoping took over as the country's leader in 1978, he immediately loosened the restraints on private business. For the first time in three decades, peasants were allowed to sell their crops in the open market, and a host of small businesses rose up to provide local services. As a student at Peking University in 1983, I would walk through the streets and see small-time entrepreneurs with their wares spread out on sheets on the sidewalks, things like shampoo, soap, cotton towels (hard to get because of cotton quotas), and children's toys. These were hardly sophisticated markets, but to Chinese starved of any commerce for decades they offered a new source of income and of consumer goods.

But it was tough for these local entrepreneurs to get their hands on capital to expand their fledgling businesses. They relied on an informal network of small lenders, everyone from family members to other people in the community. Over time, though, people formed informal financial cooperatives to lend money to aspiring businessmen and businesswomen. The amounts of capital and the businesses themselves were small-scale; even liberal Deng would not permit private entrepreneurs to challenge the state monopoly on most aspects of production. But these were the green shoots of capitalism—and the people who loaned money to them were China's first Shadow Bankers.

There was another reason for the growth of Shadow Banking. Since the beginning of China's post-Communist history, in order to create the growth the leaders were seeking, they needed a source of capital for investment. There are four ways for companies to obtain capital: loans, company profits, the state, and foreign investment. In most emerging economies, the consumer and corporate savings are the largest pools of capital for companies. The easiest and most plentiful source are the savings deposits in the banking system. Those savings can be transformed into investment capital to jumpstart the economy. This is what happened in China.

In order to capitalize on bank savings, the banks paid below market interest rates to savers. That way government-owned businesses could get their hands on cheap money—at the expense of the citizens who provided the savings deposits. This policy, known as "financial repression," provided an inexpensive pool of capital for the state-owned firms to use for investments. Nicholas Lardy, one of the leading economists on China, notes, "In effect, depositors have been taxed so that borrowers, historically mostly state-owned companies, can have access to cheap credit" (Lardy 2012). Lardy estimates that this "implicit tax" on households totaled 255 billion renminbi in 2008, 4.1 percent of GDP, and nearly three times the actual household tax imposed by the State (Lardy 2008). Shadow Banking offered a way out of this trap. *Suddenly, Shadow Banking provided a system for savers to escape the clutches of the State-run financial system.* Instead of receiving a paltry 2 percent or 3 percent on their money, they could throw it into the Shadow Banking market, and receive double or even triple that return.

Over the next several decades, China witnessed a growing population of small Shadow Banks. They took various forms including informal lending cooperatives, tiny rural "mini" banks, and even pawn shops. Eventually, the informal lenders grew to be rural cooperative banks. Each province differed in how much financial and political support they would provide to their hopeful entrepreneurs. But, with Deng Xiaoping's important support, local politicians began to allow money to flow outside of the formal banks—in the "shadows" outside of the formal banking system. They provided a key source of capital at a time, particularly in the 1980s, when China enjoyed the fastest growth since the 1949 revolution.

These informal banks were lightly regulated by the People's Bank of China (PBOC) in Beijing. The PBOC was torn between a desire to provide credit to the rural population and concern that these informal banks would go belly up—a tension that has stayed with the Chinese central bank to this day. To some extent, the PBOC purposely turned a blind eye to what was happening in the nooks and crannies of the Chinese economy. What happened with Shadow Banking in China is not completely dissimilar to the Mortgage Crisis in the USA. As former Treasury Secretary Tim Geithner said, "The money tended to flow where the regulations were weakest." The same was true of China's Shadow Banks.

The explosion in China's Shadow Banking—and where our story really begins—did not occur until decades later. In 2008, sparked by the Great Financial Crisis in the USA, the world collapsed into a recession. China's hyper-fast 10 percent plus GDP growth was under threat. Panicking, China's leaders struggled to come up with a plan to prevent the country's economic growth from backsliding, potentially throwing millions out of work, and threatening the stability of the Communist Party. They came up with a classic government solution: spend money. They told the banks to open the spigots for a fiscal stimulus the size of which the world had never witnessed. When all was said and done, China spent *4 trillion yuan* or $586 billion to accelerate the country's GDP. That compares with a mere $152 billion invested by the USA during its fiscal stimulus in 2008. The stimulus did not formally end until November 2010 although there has been significant government expenditure since then.

But there was a big problem with pumping money at the economy like water out of a firehose: the system wasn't designed to handle that much cash at once. Banks rushed to make loans to their favorite customers, mainly state-owned companies. But even the state giants in oil, steel, and industry couldn't absorb, or spend, billions of new loans in the space of a year or two. So the banks and others in the system began to rely on intermediaries to get the money spent—quickly. This is where Shadow Banking came into its own. This flood of money had to be spent. So, China cleverly allowed, or in some case invented, a host of new, even larger, Shadow Banks. The share Shadow Loans surged from less than 10 percent of the system in 2008 to almost 40 percent in 2013 (Dang et al. 2015).

As this new Shadow Banking system grew, the official banks were still under the thumb of tough regulations such as limits on the ratio of loans to deposits, along with restrictions on loans to risky industries. Compared with the Shadow Banks, the official banks were like long-distance runners running with 20-pound weights in each hand. These tight controls over bank lending forced the banks to look for new ways to generate income and feed the insatiable demand for credit among companies and local governments. Soon, they, too, jumped into Shadow Banking in new creative ways (Chen et al. 2016).

As a result, Shadow Banking continued its upward climb, even after the stimulus money dried up. The pipeline was too important for many in the system. Total credit—including banks and Shadow Banks—doubled from 6.9 trillion yuan in 2008 to 13.9 trillion in 2009. The share of Shadow Banking money jumped from 30 percent to close to 50 percent of all new loans.

The previous mom-and-pop shops and other small players in the Shadow Banking market morphed into much larger financial institutions. The Shadow Banks were actually a mix of both state and non-state institutions.

The biggest Shadow Banks were the Trusts. These odd beasts were local investment funds set up mainly by Provincial governments with some backing from private companies. Following the stimulus package in 2009, these 67 Trusts began accumulating and lending money like mad. Trusts had $200 billion in outstanding loans in 2008. That number rose by two-thirds to $330 billion in 2009, $500 billion in 2010, and by 2013 was *more than $1.8 trillion*. That's a lot of loans from a tiny group of non-banks.

Oddly enough, the other big player in the Shadow Banking business were the state banks—the Bank of China, Agricultural Bank of China, Industrial and Commercial Bank of China, and the China Construction Bank. These four state giants realized they could make some extra profits by jumping into the Shadow Banking game, and keep their customers happy by offering a host of new investment opportunities. The key difference between their investment products (or Shadow Loans) and an ordinary loan was that they could keep them off their books. Instead of a loan, with all the regulation that entailed, they treated these Shadow Loans almost like an investment banking deal that provided a quick commission. These off-balance sheet loans grew tremendously from close to zero in 2008 to more than 14 trillion renminbi (more than $2 trillion) by 2014.

These large, state-owned banks were joined by smaller banks that also saw a way continue to attract customers with high return investments.

At the time of writing in 2016, the official calculation of the size of Shadow Banking by the PBOC was 60 trillion renminbi, or 88 percent of GDP. But this didn't include a new batch of loans—coined "investments"—that were slipping through the regulatory cracks and could be considered quasi-Shadow Loans. They added another 11 trillion renminbi to the mix for a total of 71 trillion renminbi, or 118 percent of GDP. Unfortunately, the whole story of what is and is not a Shadow Loan becomes quite complicated. Throughout this book we will discuss a variety of what we consider to be lightly regulated capital flows mainly through non-bank financial actors. We will, though, include some flows that pass through the banks, and consider them to be forms of Shadow Banking.

This book is designed as an inside look into one of the greatest increases in credit the world has ever seen. But beyond size alone, there are several other key ingredients to the story that we will be touching upon.

First, although Shadow Banking has added fuel to China's debt burden, it has also contributed to the growth of capitalism in China—with a Chinese twist. Shadow Banking has provided credit to fledgling businesses since Deng's reforms in the 1980s and continues to do so today. There are recent problems with Shadow Banking and its relationship to capitalism. Much of the recent flood of money from Shadow Banks has been invested in local projects run by companies that have substantial state support. It is questionable whether these companies can really be called capitalist, even though according to Chinese regulators they are independent of the government. In addition, during the past ten years, these local businesses have acted as a kind of a fiscal piggy bank for cash-strapped local governments. These property projects and purchases of land have been an important source of revenue. This use of private wealth for fiscal ends is not favorable to capitalism, nor is it an efficient way to manage an economy.

However, Xing Libin is not the only entrepreneur who made his money thanks to Shadow Loans. There are many others across China who grew their business as a result of new channels of financing outside of the formal banks. Thousands if not millions of small business across China were able to start, grow, and even sell shares to the public as the result of the capital that Shadow Banking provided. Between 2010 and 2012, private firms received 52 percent of all bank loans compared to just 10 percent of all loans just a few decades earlier when almost all firms were state or collectively owned (Lardy, Nicholas. *Markets Over Mao*. Location 2626. Kindle

Edition). Small, private businesses had a tougher time obtaining bank loans than the state firms did. Therefore, frequently they turned to the Shadow Banks for capital. A 2012 survey of 15 provinces concluded that 57.5 percent relied on informal finance (Tsai 2016). Even Jack Ma, founder of China's version of Amazon, started his company with $20,000 in seed money from his wife and a friend—a kind of small-scale Shadow Loan.

The second point is that Shadow Banking is very much a creature of the Chinese political system. Politics dictates banking in all countries—and China is no exception. Academics Charles Calomiris and Stephen Haber note in their history of global banking crises, "Fragile by Design," banks are a product of who owns them and what rights the government gives them. "Modern banking is best thought of as a partnership between the government and a group of bankers, a partnership that is shaped by the institutions that govern the distribution of power in the political system." In China, that power has shifted between Beijing, local governments, and private entrepreneurs. Shadow Banking has been an important component of this shift (Calomiris and Haber 2014). How?

We will argue that Shadow Banking has allowed the Communist Party to allow a market economy to flourish without directly challenging state control. In recent years, capital has flowed rapidly through unofficial channels—unchecked by mandarins in Beijing. Indeed, in some cases, as we have seen with the fiscal stimulus, these flows *were actively encouraged* by the state to overcome shortcomings in the economic system that couldn't be addressed through official channels. In a sense, Shadow Banking allowed the state to paper over fiscal cracks in the system. Shadow Banking has been the glue that has tied the capitalist and non-capitalist economy together in one, rather untidy, bundle. Political scientist Kellee Tsai calls this the creation of a "parallel political economy" that has supported the state (Tsai 2015).

In our concluding sections, we will address one key question regarding the future of Shadow Banking in China. First, could Shadow Banking cause a financial collapse? The general consensus to this question is no. There are adequate resources within China's banks to handle a series of defaults in the Shadow Banking sector. There are some systemic risks to Shadow Banking, mainly in a rising group of the investments between banks. But these are probably not large enough to cause an economic collapse. The share of Shadow Banking held by Emerging Markets doubled from 2010 to 2014 to 12 percent, mostly driven by China. Still, although China is facing a debt crisis partly caused by the rapid rise in Shadow

Banking, its global share of Shadow Banking, at 4 percent, remains relatively small (Financial Stability Board 2015a). In terms of GDP, Shadow Banking in Ireland, the United Kingdom, Switzerland, and the USA stood at the high-end of the spectrum, with 1,190 percent, 147 percent, 90 percent, and 82 percent of GDP, respectively.

However, that doesn't mean that Shadow Banking won't create a crisis in China. A deflating asset bubble tied to the property market, similar to what the USA suffered during the mortgage meltdown, could lead to a serious fall in household wealth. Many individuals would pull money from the Shadow economy, accelerating the property collapse. This could migrate into declining confidence in the ability of Beijing to control its own economy, which, in turn, could escalate into a political crisis. "China is displaying the same three symptoms that Japan, the US and parts of Europe all showed before suffering financial crises: a rapid build-up of leverage, elevated property prices and a decline in potential growth" (Zhang 2013). So there are distinct risks to Shadow Banking.

Despite these caveats, we believe the future is bright for Shadow Banking in China for the simple reason that the state needs it. China's economy is slowing and, depending on the outlook, may grind almost to a halt in the near future. The main problem is an excess of debt from both banks and Shadow Banks. Our belief is that a gradual decline in available capital will shrink the opportunities for many businesses to grow using loans from the banking system. Therefore, the Shadow Banks will step in to fill the gap when the state (and the formal banks) cannot. This has been the history of Shadow Banking and is likely to accelerate under conditions of austerity. The current abuses of Shadow Banking through risky lending, such as for short-term financial gain, are likely to be curtailed by regulators, and its proper place as a source of capital for business will reemerge.

How China handles the coming downturn, and how it treats its Shadow Banks, will have an enormous impact on China and the global economy. A collapse in credit, both formal and informal, will slow the growth of the economy. A crackdown on Shadow Lenders, while curbing the excesses among greedy bankers, would also stifle the local entrepreneurs who employ millions of mainly rural residents.

Beijing is walking a tightrope between too much or too little credit. The Shadow Banks are a key part of this calculus. China must successfully integrate these financial institutions that are operating in the dim recesses of China's economy. They must slowly wean the state institutions from their dependency on state credit and allow capital to flow more freely to the more profitable companies, most of which are privately held. The success or failure of this integration will have an enormous impact on China and its relationship with the global economy. It is important for everyone, both in China and around the globe, to understand how these Shadow Banks fit into the country's financial mosaic. This book is an attempt to describe how Shadow Banking in China is having a profound effect on the country's economic growth and the rise of capitalism.

CHAPTER 2

Early Shoots of Informal Finance

When I was a student at Peking University in 1983, I would walk through the main campus square on my way to class and see dozens of traders selling their wares spread out on large cotton sheets spread out on the dusty concrete. You could buy anything, from scissors, thread, small bars of soap—a variety of daily necessities. At the time it did not strike me as unusual for an emerging market. But for China it was revolutionary. These small businessmen and businesswomen had only been allowed to exist since 1979—a scant four years. They were China's first capitalists, and Shadow Banking played a crucial role. This incipient capitalism was all due to one man: Deng Xiao Ping.

When Deng became China's paramount leader in 1979, he was in a quandary. He was struggling to negotiate between groups in the country who had opposing ideas of how to modernize the economy. This was a crucial moment for Deng. He had slavishly followed Mao Zedong's erratic policies for decades, including the disastrous Cultural Revolution, which almost ground China's economy to a halt as private business was banned and all economic activity was funneled through state institutions such as giant farming cooperatives. But with Mao's death in 1976, and the overthrow of his wife Jiang Qing and her colleagues who had led the Cultural Revolution, Deng finally freed himself from the political and economic handcuffs that had tied the country down for so long. He was nearly unanimously selected to run the country. But he still had to contend with conflicting views on where China should go.

© The Author(s) 2017
A. Collier, *Shadow Banking and the Rise of Capitalism in China*,
DOI 10.1007/978-981-10-2996-7_2

Although he was 75, Deng was in good shape. According to a biography by the Russian scholar Alexander Pantsov and the American Steven Levine, in July 1979, Deng climbed a famous mountain in Anhui province called Huangshan, spending three days enjoying the views. "The lesson of Huangshan is that I am fully up to the standards," he told a colleague (Pantsov and Levine 2015).

What was the struggle? Essentially, between the "Old Guard" who had founded the People's Republic of China in 1949 and a newer group of leaders who believed that it was time for China to take a different path. The conflict was primarily between Hu Yaobang, a reformer and one of the youngest members of the famous Long March that took Mao to power, and supporters of the Old Guard including Deng Liqun, a pro-Maoist intellectual who a decade later vigorously defended the crackdown on the demonstrators in the Tiananmen incident. There was also lingering power held by Hua Guofeng, Mao's chosen successor and a hardliner, and Chen Yun, a trained economist who was somewhat more moderate in his views. Hu also found himself up against the even more reform-minded Zhao Ziyang.

The big question was one China has been struggling with since its founding in 1949: Should the state control the economy or should there be gradual loosening of controls over economic activity? For Deng, although he was eager to increase incomes to the country's impoverished people, he also had to strike a balance between the different groups. But the disputes were as much about turf battles as they were about policy. Political scientist Susan Shirk argues that during this period the struggle for control over resources turf between bureaucracies was one of the key dynamics.

In her view, the fundamental schism was not between reformers and non-reformers. This is the analytic line that the Western observers take because it fits within the Western framework of Democratic Capitalism. The better way to think of these early, crucial conflicts is to look at three factors. First, which bureaucracies would be winners and losers under any reform plan; second, what were the more technical arguments over which plan would be better for the economy; and third, how would these conflicts affect the heated competition between Hu Yaobang and Zhao Ziyang about who would be Deng's successor. The economy became a cudgel in the debate (Shirk 1993).

***

In Shirk's view, there were two alternative approaches to fixing China's ailing state corporations—what she terms enterprise reform. One was called "profit contracting," and the other was tax reform. "The debate between these two approaches began to divide the ranks of pro reform economists and officials," she notes (Shirk, Chapter on Leadership Succession).

Tax for profit, being pushed by Zhao Ziyang, would have permitted Beijing to allocate capital generated by the state sector to firms according to their level of profitability. This plan would force the state firms to improve efficiency more rapidly because profits would be the telling factor. The more hardline (and hidebound) Hu Yaobang favored contracting—which essentially gave fixed targets to each state sector, leaving more wiggle room for bargaining between bureaucrats—and more pork for supporters. In this strategy, profits would take a back seat. As Shirk states, "Hu's greatest political resource was his national network of clients. He needed to keep this faction well-fed by distributing patronage. Particularistic contracting was a kind of Chinese 'pork', special favors that politicians such as Hu could hand out to their followers" (Shirk, Chapter on Leadership Succession).

Zhao won. In 1983, the State Council approved tax-for-profit over profit-contracting, a victory that surprised the more pro-Capitalist reformers.

More broadly, Victor Shih, a Professor of Political Economy at the University of California in San Diego, believes the underlying power dynamic among the elite in China can be seen through the lens of factional politics. "Top Chinese leaders perpetually face threats to their power due to the lack of an institutionalize succession mechanism and the dearth of clear indicators of power. To mitigate this uncertainty, the leaders form factions, which are composed of a loose group of lower officials who have an incentive to provide political support to top leaders in times of political challenges" (Shih 2008). These factions are formed over their careers through common jobs, geographical base, or home territory. Although his focus in the book is on the fight against inflation, this analytical framework can be applied to the debates over Shadow Banking. Which institutions are allowed to lend capital and which groups are permitted to borrow it?

We've strayed a bit far from the theme of Shadow Banking. But it's important to at least touch upon the role of state reform—and elite dynamics—at a crucial juncture in China's modern history. This helps lay the groundwork to explain how capital was allocated in subsequent decades, how capitalism took shape, and where Shadow Banking fits into the picture. Without gradual (and still incomplete) reform of the state sector, Shadow Banking would have taken a different tack.

Now, we turn to the earliest seeds of Shadow Banking—or informal finance as it is known in its embryonic stage—in China's heartland.

***

When Deng Xiao Ping instituted the economic reforms that electrified China's economy, he had to find a way to pay for them. Where would the money come for local businesses? After all, this was a Communist State. Until Deng's reforms were launched in 1979, Beijing allocated credit through the central bank directly to State firms. Local governments had their own sources of revenue that they also divided out to State firms. The PBOC was the only bank in the People's Republic of China and was responsible for both central banking and commercial banking operations. The other banks in the system were what are called "policy banks"—they acted as arms of the central bank by allocating credit to their respective areas of expertise, such as agriculture or industry. In 1983, China began creating a fully fledged banking system by separating the four policy banks into independent entities. These were the Bank of China, the Construction Bank of China, the Industrial and Commercial Bank of China, and the Agricultural Bank of China. They did not become fully separated (although they are still three-quarters owned by the central government) until the early 2000s, when the banks hived off their bad loans and sold shares to the public through the Hong Kong Stock Exchange.

There are many facets to Deng's liberalization that are too difficult to describe in one short summary. However, a key aspect of the economic changes, and one that is an important explanation for the rise of Shadow Banking, was something called "financial repression." This became one of Beijing's top ways of paying for economic growth.

First coined in 1973 by American economists Edward Shaw and Ronald McKinnon, financial repression refers to a series of economic policies that provides lower rates of return to savers than under a free market system. These policies could include lower interest rates, abnormally high liquidity ratios, high bank reserve requirements, capital controls, restrictions on market entry into the financial sector, credit ceilings or restrictions on credit allocation, and government ownership of banks. In the end, in the view of free market economists, these policies discourage savings and investment because the rates of return are lower than in a competitive market. But they also can provide a cheap source of credit for the state for whatever aims it deems important. Let's take a simple example. A local entrepreneur launches a business making soap. He expects a return on his investment of 12 percent per year. He borrows money from the bank at 6 percent, giving him plenty of room for healthy profits.

Where does he get his startup capital? From the banks. In a Western economy, the banks may pay savers 5 percent, giving them a small profit of 1 percent. However, in China, the banks pay savers much less—as little as 2 percent. That spread gives the banks a huge profit margin. Multiply that across all of China's banks and you're talking about trillions of renminbi in profits that pour into bank coffers like water down a drain spout in a rainstorm.

Financial repression is difficult to engineer in a free market economy with a competitive banking system and developed financial markets. How do you force people to hand over their savings to a banking system that pays low returns when you can simply take your money to the stock market? However, China didn't have this problem. There was hardly any domestic stock market to speak of. The international markets were closed off to domestic residents because of China's tight restrictions on access to foreign exchange. There was some informal lending through unofficial institutions such as Shadow Banks, which we will discuss in more detail, but for the most part these did not account—at least in the early days—for substantial portions of credit. That left the banks. Savers knew the banks were safe because they were owned by the government. And the state banks had many branches throughout China. Even after decades of reform, in 2012 the five state banks controlled 49 percent of total assets and employed 1.7 million people across the country. And in the early days of economic reform in 1996, the state banks had 153,070 branches compared with just 3,748 for all of the other banks combined. They owned the economy.

This system gave Beijing carte blanche over the country's savings. It's as if the people of China woke up one day and handed their savings to the government. And these savings were quite plentiful. In December 2015, there were 20.6 trillion renminbi in household deposits or 14.9 percent of total deposits of 137.9 trillion. Deposit rates at one bank, the Bank of China, that year ranged between 0.3 percent and 2.75 percent, depending on how long you left the money in the bank. In contrast, in October 2015, the benchmark one-year lending rate was 4.35 percent. That spread of around 2 percentage points was a boon to the banks and, ultimately, to the state. The banks were earning approximately 2 percent, or 420 billion renminbi, on 21 trillion renminbi per year.

Economist Nicholas Lardy of the Peterson Institute in Washington has long studied this issue. In one paper, he noted that in 2002, the PBOC set demand deposit rates at 0.72 percent. Meanwhile, inflation started to rack up big gains, rising from just 0.8 percent in 2002 to 8 percent in 2008. That meant that banks were providing savers with a *negative return* of more than 7 percent; they were losing significant ground on their money. They were basically handing over cash to the state (Lardy 2008).

Who were the beneficiaries of this financial largess? According to Lardy, financial repression costs Chinese households about 255 billion renminbi (US$36 billion), 4.1 percent of China's GDP, with one-fifth going to corporations, one-quarter to banks, and the government taking the rest.

Yiping Huang, a Professor of Economics at Peking University, notes that financial repression has stifled economic growth by giving cheap capital to inefficient industries. After all, if the banks were getting cheap money, they could lend without paying much attention to the profitability of the borrowers. Professor Huang estimated that financial repression held down per capita GDP growth by 3.0–3.6 percentage points in 1978 and by 1.7–2.1 percentage points in 2008. With financial liberalization starting with Deng's reforms, GDP has been increased by 1.3–1.5 percentage points per year, compared to 30 years ago (Huang and Wang 2010).

Huang constructed an index of financial repression, looking at six areas: (1) negative real interest rates, (2) interest rate controls, (3) capital account regulations, (4) statutory reserve requirement, (5) public sector share of bank deposits, and (6) public sector share of bank loans. He calculated that the financial repression index fell from 1.0 in 1978 to 0.58 in 2008. This decline by 42 percent is strong evidence that China has come a long way to liberalize its economy.

More recently, Lardy has examined the flows of capital to private and State firms and calculated the impact of differing interest rates, which is one measure of financial repression. He notes that a joint survey of more than 100 Chinese financial institutions by the People's Bank of China and the International Finance Corporation in 2004–2005 showed that the average interest rate charged to state-owned companies, 5.67 percent, was only slightly below the average of 5.96 percent charged to privately owned companies. A survey of over 5000 registered private firms in 2011 reveals that little has changed. The survey found that the median interest rate paid by private firms on their bank loans was 7.8 percent, only slightly above the 7.5 percent average bank lending rate. Private firms, however, did pay somewhat more, 8 percent, for borrowings from small-scale financial institutions: rural banks, rural credit cooperatives, and micro-finance companies.

Certainly financial repression has declined over time as Beijing liberalized the financial markets. The interest rate differential is good evidence of this financial marketization. Nonetheless, financial repression has been a long-standing issue in China, exacting a significant toll on Chinese citizens' wealth, and continues in one form or another to this day.

Why is financial repression important for Shadow Banking? When credit is controlled primarily by state institutions that obtain their capital from forced savings from citizens, inevitably there is demand among citizens for other investment opportunities. This is where Shadow Banking comes into play. As Professor Kellee Tsai of Hong Kong University of Science and Technology noted:

> Financial repression—meaning governmental suppression of interest rates below market levels—represents a core feature of China's reform-era growth. In effect, household savings earning low rates of interest have been transferred through the banking system to supply subsidized credit to SOEs, capital-intensive industry, and real estate developers. The private sector's resulting reliance on informal finance is worth detailing because it represents a complementary, yet under-analyzed out-growth of state capitalism. (Tsai 2015b)

Particularly in the early years, as Beijing marshaled credit for its own policies and favored institutions, funneling most of it to the large state firms, small businessmen were starved of capital and savers weren't making reasonable returns. In one World Bank survey, only 20 percent of firm financing came from the banks, comparable to India and Indonesia. Informal finance supplied 43 percent of firm financing in China compared to less than 9 percent in other developing countries (Ayyagari et al. 2007). As we will discuss later, internal funds—profits—were the largest source of capital for small firms, accounting for all capital for 40 percent of firms surveyed (Tanaka and Monar 2008).

Shadow Banking was an escape hatch for the state. Beijing could generate income from financial repression through the official banking system while allowing leakage of capital to the private sector through Shadow Banking—particularly if the leakage led to economic growth and employment and did not threaten the primacy of the State. It was a dance acceptable to both the Chinese state and emerging Chinese capitalists.

* * *

The formative years of Shadow Banking were like the struggles of rock 'n roll during the days of swing dance bands; nobody knew what the music was—but they sure liked it.

Shadow Banking during the 1980s was marked by trial and error because households and the upper echelons of government were trying to come to grips with what the new economy really was. How much control should Beijing wield over the economy? Should the banks lend to small businesses? Should the state giants in Beijing control corporate activity? Should households be allowed to start businesses? All these questions were being debated throughout China and no one had a clear answer—including Deng himself. Deng was famous for his pragmatism as expressed in the quote, "It doesn't matter if the cat is black or yellow, as long as it can catch mice it is a good cat" (Ibid., Pantsov, p. 222).

One thing did become clear: small households would need capital if they were to expand beyond selling the occasional bok choy or cotton trousers in a street stall. However, it wasn't clear whether these small business start-ups would be a part of the socialist economy or would be completely on their own—in essence, private firms.

There has long been an intense debate among scholars about something as basic as the difference between a private and a state firm in China. Can it be defined by source of capital? Ownership? Licensing? Independence from government? For example, in the early days of economic reforms, many private companies were launched under the guise of state licenses; these were the so-called Red Hat firms. But it's unclear how independent they really were. They may have utilized private capital but obtained contracts through their government connections. Or they were managed privately but operated in a government-owned factory.

Shadow Banking has played a role in this debate, too. Deng's strong march into free market economics had an impact not only on business but also on banking. The state banks had become accustomed to their comfortable role lending to state firms. Why go to all the trouble of assessing a company's credit, or the profitability of a new factory, when you can lend to a firm that you know will be supported by the government? It's much easier to take an official out to a karaoke bar and settle the loan over glasses of grain alcohol and platters of spicy chicken.

However, the new economic system required a new set of credit intermediaries. Thus, were spawned the first Shadow Banks.

It's hard to estimate the size of Shadow Banking in the 1980s and early 1990s. The data is very sparse. Jianjun Li of the Central University of Finance and Economics (CUFE) in Beijing and Sara Hsu of the State University of New York in New Paltz estimate that as many as 30 percent of rural households and 56 percent of self-employed households were involved in private lending. Shuxia Jiang, of Xiamen University, cites a survey in 1999 that estimated that more than 75 percent of the debt of rural households came from informal financial sources (Li and Shu 2009).

There were a number of informal sources of credit in China in the early days. These included local associations that provided a pool of credit, called credit associations. There have been three types of early associations: rotating associations, which gathered funds and then allocated the total pot of loans to each individual in turn; bidding associations, where participants bid for loans; and finally outright pyramid schemes, which were blatantly illegal. Later on, starting around 1994, there were microfinance companies, which played minor role in unofficial financial channels in China until the recent advent of online finance, when these channels shot up in size.

Shuxia Jiang of Xiamen University notes the following early, informal "Shadow" Banks:

Private Lending Among Farmers Early surveys suggest private credit between farmers accounted for 68.8 percent of all rural loans, with most of this run along standard lines of agreed upon interest rates.

Pawnbrokers Most farmers had few assets to use as collateral, but there has been a long history of pawnbroking in China, stretching back to the country's early history. Initially, the government encouraged Temples to establish pawnshops, and these gradually become more common among private individuals.

Rotating Savings and Credit Associations These were typical local credit systems that relied on village and family structures. These consist of a group of individuals who band together to make regular contributions to a common fund, and then give each member in turn access to that capital.

Money Houses The most common variant was a loan broker who functioned as an intermediary between lenders and borrowers and earns a commission for the transaction. By the time of the Chinese Revolution in 1949, there were more than 1,000 money houses in China. According to Jiang's research, after the Revolution, the money houses were transformed over four stages into financial intermediaries jointly operated with the government. By 1953, they were finally absorbed into the PBOC (Ibid., *Evolution of Informal Finance*).

University of Toronto scholar Lynette Ong has documented the rise of the most important source of capital in China's early reform years. China's industrialization in the 1980s and 1990s had been driven primarily by local government-owned firms, known as Township and Village Enterprises (TVEs). They were funded by the state-owned banks and accounted for the majority of bank loans. Ong points out that until the mid-1990s, collective enterprises employed between half- and three-quarters of the total workforce in the sector. They also received more than 90 percent of total bank loans throughout the 1980s and the first half of the 1990s. Over time, with the reforms put into place in the late 1990s by Premier Zhu Rongji, and the beginnings of privately owned businesses, the TVE's control of bank loans declined. In one town in Sichuan province, the collective TVEs, which had the closest connections to the government, fell from 60 percent of the total TVEs in 1985 to only 1 percent in 2002. Likewise, their share of bank loans fell from 89 percent to 34 percent (Ong 2012).

As bank loans declined, the winners in the access-to-capital sweepstakes were the private and household businesses. And right alongside of them came the informal financial institutions. These were China's first official (if we can call them official) Shadow Banks, called rural credit cooperatives (RCCs). The RCCs provided a source of credit to rural farmers. They were encouraged to provide farmer loans to increase agricultural production because Deng could clearly see that the agricultural sector had lagged behind during Mao's many political experiments. The capital also was used to form new businesses. As Ong notes, "Owing to their monopoly position in rural China, the RCCs are critical to lifting household income, stimulating the growth of small and medium-sized enterprises." They held almost 80 percent of farmer's savings and provided the same amount in loans (Ibid., *Prosper or Perish*).

As with many Shadow Banks in China, the RCCs had to play a dual role. They were stuck in the middle between the state and free markets.

They provided credit to the private sector, primarily farmers and small business, but also funneled money to the newly created TVEs. These TVEs were supposed to be the green shoots of private enterprise in China, a form of free market entrepreneurship under the tutelage of the government. The majority of these firms were collective enterprises run by local authorities—usually badly. These were generally failed experiments. Much of the money deposited by rural farmers in the RCCs were borrowed by these TVEs, which often used the money for pet projects of the local governments. According to Ong's estimates, more than 80 percent of the TVE loans eventually defaulted, squandered by clueless local government officials (Ibid., *Prosper or Perish*).

Still, the RCCs were an experiment, and the government kept a close eye on them—or at least tried to. In the early days, the RCCs were forced to report to the Agricultural Bank of China. Over time, though, the RCCs' political oversight kept changing, an example of the confusing nature of the early days of Shadow Banking.

By the early 2000s, nearly half of the 35,000 RCCs were insolvent. Eventually, the central government was forced to inject 650 billion yuan into the RCCs to keep them from collapsing. But they soon almost disappeared from the map—the first major casualty of the Shadow Banking wars. They popped up again briefly in 2013. The China Banking Regulatory Commission (CBRC) encouraged local agricultural offices to allow farmers who knew one another to cooperate on financing and product. By the middle of 2013, 137 coops had been established in one town alone, Yancheng, Jiangsu province, with deposits of 2.3 billion renminbi. But instead of lending to farmers, many coops shifted into riskier forms of lending, serving small factory owners and real estate developers who often cannot obtain bank loans. As a result, the coops' 80 billion renminbi of loans defaulted (Reuters 2014).

***

As Deng's reforms took hold in the 1980s and into the 1990s, there continued to be pockets of local credit formation. For example, in 1987, 300,000 people were involved in money lending in Wenzhou City, an economically aggressive region in Zhejiang province facing Taiwan, with as much as 1.2 billion renminbi in outstanding loans. But many of these lenders collapsed, leaving 80,000 farming households deep in debt, according to Shuxia Jiang's research (Ibid., Jiang, *The Evolution of Informal Finance*). By 1992, nearly 40 percent of the capital for private enterprise came from informal banks, almost double their credit received from the formal state banks. Later surveys in 2002 indicated that informal credit accounted for 5 percent of the deposits in the official banks and 7 percent of their operating capital (Ibid., *The Evolution of Informal Finance*). In the city of Wenzhou, a dynamic zone of entrepreneurs in Fujian province, it was estimated that in the period 1983–1985, informal financing constituted 95 percent of total capital flows (Liu 1992).

The CBRC did allow domestic firms and residents to set up micro-credit firms in 2006. According to the PBOC, the mainland had 3,366 micro-credit firms by the end of June 2011 with outstanding loans of 287.5 billion renminbi. Although this was a bold step in liberalizing the lending market, small-loan firms have been required to comply with rigid rules such as having a registered capital of no less than 50 million renminbi, taking no deposits from residents or firms, and offering loans at interest rates a maximum of four times rates set by the central bank (Shen 2012).

Despite these early variants of informal lending, the formal banks still dominated China's economy. And the bulk of credit in China's financial system was allocated to the state companies. They were the ones considered to be the backbone of China's economy. In 1985, more than one-fifth of China's official state budget were invested in state firms. Around the same time, bank credit financed about 20 percent of all investment (Lardy 2008).

* * *

While the early days of Shadow Banking were marked by failures, with credit cooperatives and other financial intermediaries collapsing, they also provided the foundations of capitalism in China. The state was toying with capitalism—and Shadow Banks were important participants. But the leadership didn't always know what they were doing. They experimented. Later, Deng Xiaoping made this his mantra. "We should be bolder than before in conducting reform and opening up to the outside and have the courage to experiment," he said during his famous 1992 trip to southern China to encourage modernization. In the early days of reform, it was much of a free-for-all, and finance was a big part of the experimentation. It was like young children playing a toss-up game of soccer; there was no field and no official referee, but the players took the game seriously.

As we shall see, over time, Shadow Banking increasingly operated on its own, separate from the experiments by the leadership. In fact, in recent years, Shadow Banking has become like the snake being swallowed by a pig—the pig (Shadow Banks) became so big they almost kill the snake. We now jump forward in time to the Great Financial Crisis in 2007, when Shadow Banking really took off.

CHAPTER 3

China's Great Financial Push

In 2008, China faced a crisis. The American mortgage meltdown and the global slowdown threatened China's double-digit GDP growth. Suddenly, after years of chalking up huge economic gains, China was like a long-distance runner fighting a headwind. The leadership in Beijing, accustomed to sitting back and letting the economy roar, was suddenly concerned. In an article in 2010 for the East Asia Forum, Yu Yongding, an economist at the Chinese Academy of Social Sciences, the leadership's think tank in Beijing, described the sense of panic:

> In the second half of 2008, export demand collapsed due to the global financial crisis. Long-postponed overcapacity surfaced suddenly. The sudden shift from inflation to deflation, in September to October 2008 was truly stunning. (East Asia Forum 2010)

The leadership could see alarming trends. For decades the economy had been quite strong. China's exports as a share of GDP rose from 9.1 percent in 1985 to 37.8 percent in 2008, surpassing the USA and second only to Germany, contributing one-third of its GDP growth. Then, exports dropped like a stone. After rising 25 percent in September 2007, exports suddenly shrank by 2.2 percent in November and were in a position to reduce the country's GDP by 3 percent, according to Yongding's analysis.

Along with structural issues threatening growth, the Great Financial Crisis (GFC) could cause significant problems for China. Initially, Chinese

© The Author(s) 2017
A. Collier, *Shadow Banking and the Rise of Capitalism in China*,
DOI 10.1007/978-981-10-2996-7_3

authorities saw the Shadow Banking system as the fundamental cause of the GFC in the West, of which China was a victim (Zheng 2015). They did not want to be infected by what they saw as a Western problem. But there was also concern that the GFC could exacerbate existing structural problems within the Chinese economy.

So the policymakers reacted. As the Oxford-trained Professor Yu said, "With or without the GFC, overcapacity and the need for correction were inevitable. The global economic crisis merely exposed the vulnerability of China's growth pattern in a dramatic fashion. The Chinese government moved quickly to mitigate falling GDP growth after the GFC through a stimulus package and monetary expansion" (East Asia Forum 2010).

Internally, Chinese leaders had long been worried about avoiding a Soviet-style collapse. In the Chinese view, this would result from a combination of lack of support for the Chinese Communist Party, coupled with a sharp slowdown in economic growth. In a speech in 2012, President Xi Jinping evoked these fears when he cited the Soviet Union in an internal speech. "Gorbachev announced the disbandment of the Soviet Communist Party in a blithe statement. A big Party was gone just like that. Proportionally, the Soviet Communist Party had more members than we do, but nobody was man enough to stand up and resist" (China Digital Times, January 27, 2013).

These worries extended not just to the Party and to the military, but also to the financial system. In the minds of senior leaders, widespread economic chaos could lead to the breakdown of the Chinese Communist Party, the bedrock of the Chinese political system. That's why the financial crisis caused such shivers in Beijing.

Despite its reputation as a tightly controlled, closed economy, China has a striking ability to react to events, both global and domestic. Beijing's political antennae are finely attuned to the shifts in policy emanating from the world's financial and political centers. The country does not always react in ways that other countries would agree with. And most events are filtered through China's intense domestic politics. But there is no doubt that the leadership and the senior bureaucrats are aware of changing global and domestic trends.

China was not completely unprepared for a global crisis. The country had suffered through the Asian Financial Crisis of 1997 and had seen how countries such as Thailand that had been deeply exposed to global capital flows had suddenly seen the money—and the economic growth—flutter away in the breeze, as investors withdrew their capital.

China's response was to inject massive amounts of cash into the economy. In November 2008, the government introduced a 4 trillion yuan stimulus package—14 percent of 2008 GDP—for 2009 and 2010. That package ultimately raised 12 trillion renminbi in funds through a variety of sources, both state and private. This US$1.8 trillion package was less than the US$7 trillion the USA committed to the economy at the height of the mortgage crisis in 2008 and 2009. But much of the US assistance came in the form of guarantees and other support, not just loans and capital injections. China's package was in the form of loans—basically cash. The money was handed out so quickly it was reminiscent of the famous comment by economist Milton Friedman that the best way to stimulate an economy running below capacity was to drop money from a helicopter.

The decision to inject capital into the economy was made by the 35-member State Council presided by then-Premier Wen Jiabao. Xinhua News Agency said the country would "loosen credit conditions, cut taxes, and embark on a massive infrastructure spending program" (Xinhua 2008). The 4 trillion renminbi program would be spent over ten years to finance key programs in ten major areas, including low-income housing, rural infrastructure, water, electricity, and transportation. There also would be a 120 billion renminbi reduction in value-added taxes to spur industrial growth. The entire package would total 8 percent of China's 2009 GDP of $4.9 trillion—more than the 6.8 percent of US 2008 GDP, or $1 trillion, that the USA spent. The stimulus was large because "China drew lessons from the Asian Financial Crisis in 1998," according to Jia Kang, director of the Research Institute for Fiscal Sciences at the Ministry of Finance (China.org.cn, November 10, 2008). The stimulus rose to 13 percent of GDP. In the end, including other investments, overall expenditure by the state in things like bridges, roads, and property was a whopping 48 percent of GDP from 2009 to 2012.

Not surprisingly, as local governments rushed to spend money, local property values boomed. From 2001 to 2008, the proceeds from land sales, on average, were 40.5 percent of local government income, but they jumped to 61 percent of income during the two years of the stimulus package as governments took advantage of the flood of money (Fabre 2013).

The major difference between the Chinese stimulus and the US version was that the American response was designed to prop up the banks, reduce their high-risk investment banking and trading operations, and force them to go back to their basic function—making loans to businesses. In contrast, China's response was to use the banks to make direct fiscal injections into the economy; essentially, use the banks to force credit where the state wanted it. The difference between the two countries' response to the crisis was striking. The American policy was like opening the gates of a dam to control a flood; China's policies were designed to alter the course of the river itself.

The State Council's decision to roll out the US$586 billion stimulus package "ramped up expenditures on affordable housing, rural and other infrastructure (highways, railways and airports), public health and education, the environment and technical innovation," according to Nicholas Lardy of the Peterson Institute (Ibid., China's Economic Growth After the Global Financial Crisis, p. 5). Lardy sees the Chinese policies to the crisis differing from the US response in two respects: China relied on fiscal expenditures, basically spending money directly on goods and services. In contrast, one-third of the US action consisted of indirect stimulus through tax cuts. In addition, the USA under Treasury Secretary Tim Geithner paid down debt rather than increasing demand.

As the result of monetary easing through interest rate cuts and fiscal injections, China witnessed a large increase in lending. Domestic currency loans jumped by 7.4 trillion renminbi in the first half of 2009, triple the size of the increase a year earlier. It appears that these loans were highly effective for economic growth. GDP bottomed out in the end of 2008, when economic growth slowed to 4.3 percent, but jumped to 11.4 percent by the middle of 2009 as the stimulus kicked in. China could proudly point to its success in averting a financial crisis that had simultaneously hit most other major nations in the world. But there were doubts even then about how all this would end up.

As the head of American operations for the investment bank of the Bank of China, I witnessed the huge jump in investment in China during this period, much of it wasteful. Once during a trip to the city of Xian, home of the Terracotta Warriors, I and a group of fund managers were escorted by a van around town by my colleagues. "There's the new highway and the new stadium," a Bank of China employee said. "What events do you hold there?" I asked. "Oh, we have only had one event in the past year," she replied.

But like many massive government programs, the stimulus would have significant unintended consequences. China would be grappling with the impact of the massive flood of cash for years to come—and Shadow Banking was one of the big consequences.

* * *

The stimulus was less and less effective over time. There was too much money chasing too few good projects. The money was going somewhere—but not showing up on the ground. Annual real growth in gross capital formation fell to 6.6 percent in 2014, down from 10.2 percent in 2013 and a peak of 25 percent in 2009. Capital formation measures the value of acquisitions of new or existing plant and equipment. Accounting for depreciation, which is the decline in value of equipment over time due to usage, fixed capital formation may have been negative.

Some economists view the stimulus as having been good for China. Peterson Institute economist Nicholas Lardy believes China's stimulus measures maintained GDP growth while avoiding the negative consequences of a sharp downturn. He refutes many of the critiques of China's stimulus, focusing on four points: excessive bank loans, investment in excess industrial capacity, fiscal unsustainability, and the rise of the state instead of economic reform (Lardy, Sustaining China's Economic Growth, Chap. 11).

On the first point, bank lending, some analysts say the increase in loans caused excessive debt. However, Lardy notes that public and household debt on the eve of the crisis in 2007 was just 160 percent of GDP. This compares to 350 percent in the USA. So China had ample room, in his view, to issue more loans as a stimulus. On new capacity in industries that already had overcapacity, he says that investment in industries such as steel had lagged in the past. Also, most of the stimulus was not targeted at expanding production in outdated industries such as steel, but in other areas, such as property. In his discussion about whether the stimulus led to an unsustainable financial system, this goes to the question of how much debt a country can incur without a crisis. But in his view "it is likely that over the medium and long term the real economic returns to the economy as a whole on many of these infrastructure investments will be high" (Sustaining China's Economic Growth, p. 31).

These points are hotly debated among economists. One thing most economists would agree on is that the stimulus caused a huge boom in Shadow Banking. All that money going into the economy was like a fountain during a rainstorm; so much water coming down means that it will inevitably flood the fountain—and there were many Shadow Banks perfectly willing to catch the overflow.

***

The key to understanding the impact of the stimulus on Shadow Banking was how this expansionary policy was financed. The PBOC mandated that only 29 percent of the 4 trillion stimulus would be funded by the central government budget; the remaining funds would come from other sources. But who? There wasn't a lot of spare capital lying around. In the end, the central government essentially left it up to the provinces to find the additional capital. The only sources would be among the three: local governments, local corporations, and private citizens. However, this is a highly unusual form of fiscal policy. Generally, when a country needs government money to get a country back on its feet, it is paid for by the central government—not a hodgepodge of funds from central, local, and private sources. Think of how this type of stimulus would look in the USA. In the middle of a huge financial crisis, the Treasury Secretary announces a plan to boost consumption through massive government intervention. However, Washington would pay for *less than a third* of the total bill. Texas, New York, Wyoming, and every other state in the union would pick up most of the tab. There would be protests from every local township and legislature across America. (We're ignoring here tax cuts, which provide extra cash in consumer pockets and encourage them to spend.)

However, China differs markedly from the USA, and many European countries, in an important area: the extent of local responsibility for government spending. More than 70 percent of all government expenditure in China is made by sub-national governments. Many fiscal decisions are made by provincial governments and townships, not by Beijing. Beijing said to spend—but the cities and towns across China had to figure out a way to do this.

So basically it was up to the local governments to come up with the money for this massive fiscal injection. Could they do it? We must first understand how the financial relationship works between the provinces and Beijing. Only then can we get to the bottom of modern-day Shadow Banking in China. We will discuss this in the following chapter on Federalism.

***

Before we end our discussion of the fiscal stimulus, and its impact on the growth of Shadow Banking, it would be helpful to touch briefly on one long-standing debate among economists about the degree of state control over economic activity in China. And more importantly, how to measure it. Is it by looking at bank loans from state banks? Ownership of businesses? Capital structure?

Why is this important in a discussion of Shadow Banking? Shadow Banks by definition are financial intermediaries operating outside of the formal banking system. They exist in a gray area between the state—which controls much of the money in China—and the private sector. Shadow Banking traditionally has acted as a way station—a kind of a monetary shuttle bus—between the State and the market economy. Understanding the debate about this gray area is helpful in looking at the broader environment in which Shadow Banking rose to prominence.

Nicholas Lardy's opinion is that traditional patterns of capital allocation were relatively unchanged by the stimulus package; small, private business benefitted as much as the big state giants. Therefore, the stimulus did not alter existing economic relations.

Others aren't so sure. Kellee Tsai at the Hong Kong University of Science and Technology, argues that narrow definitions of state capitalism according to bank loans alone fail to take into account the intrusive presence of the Chinese Government in China's overall economic activity. "In studies of comparative capitalism, state capitalism is an analytical category that describes the hybrid organization of an economy by delineating the political motives, institutional scope, and intended effects of state intervention," she writes (Book Review, *Markets over Mao*, p. 147, Asia Policy, Number 20, July 2015). The institutions in which the private and public sector function are inevitably state directed, which heavily influences the outcome of state activity. She notes that the Party dominates the financial sector, and many significant private firms have originated from close ties to the State (computer giant Lenovo and network equipment company Huawei among them). "China's market is being mediated, even thwarted, by a host of competing political priorities—namely, social stability and the continuation of CCP rule," she says (Ibid., p. 147).

In a review of Lardy's book, *Markets Over Mao*, Yukon Huang of the Carnegie Endowment agrees with Tsai that "the state continues to play an outsized role in influencing the behavior of economic entities"

(Ibid., book Review, *Markets Over Mao*, p. 153). This has occurred mainly through the institutional arrangements in which private firms operate— not just direct state ownership. In other words, a firm needs connections with government employees to earn revenue, either to obtain government contracts or to obtain permission to access resources directly or indirectly controlled by the state.

My trips in China for the Bank of China certainly disclosed examples of the blurring of state and private activity. During a visit to Fujian province, I heard my colleagues go on at length about how they were ordered by senior officials in Beijing to lend only according to the efficiency of the project, similar to Western standards of banking. They were under pressure to improve profits, and good loans generated better profits. However, they then led me into a meeting with one of the largest state firms in Fujian, an energy giant with tentacles in many other sectors of the economy. As we left, I asked my colleagues whether the firm would be granted additional loans. I was told, "Oh, we'll lend them any thing they want. They're owned by government!" Clearly, free market principals fell by the wayside when it came to firms with state connections.

The banks frequently are caught in the middle of this dance between the state and the private sector. One example occurred with the stimulus. In traditional Western economics, a stimulus is implemented through monetary or fiscal policy. Monetary policy includes lowering interest rates or, as we saw recently in the USA, "quantitative easing" through the purchase of financial products from banks to increase the money supply. Fiscal stimulus refers to lower taxes or higher government deficits. In China, this distinction is blurred. Any monetary stimulus, including lowering interest rates or reducing bank Reserve Rate Requirements (RRR), allows new capital to flow into the economy. But this capital must be intermediated by banks (and some non-bank financials), which are political agents responsible to different actors in the system. State banks report both to the PBOC and the Ministry of Finance, and also to some degree to provincial officials. City and commercial banks have local city officials to answer to and so on…. Thus, the distinction between monetary policy and fiscal policy is blurred; these banks often use monetary stimulus for government ends.

The banks have become the central nexus for negotiations between different political groups. In general, it's fair to say that the State Council and provincial governments are intent on increasing investment. However, the PBOC and CBRC are concerned with excess debt and asset bubbles.

In addition, the stimulus fostered the growth of a relatively new economic actor, the local government financing vehicle (LGFV), that was an unusual hybrid between the state and the private sector. We will discuss the role of the LGFV in Shadow Banking further on, but it's helpful to note that this economic actor played an important role in the stimulus and Shadow Banking and has had a foot in both private and governmental economic activities.

In any case, this was perhaps a long digression into some very complicated issues about state control and capitalism in China. This is important, though, because we argue throughout this book that Shadow Banking is one of the tools China uses to bridge the gap between private and state activities. We need to have a basic grasp of the debates over this issue if we are to come to any meaningful conclusions.

CHAPTER 4

Federalism

Chongqing is the capital of Sichuan province, home of some of China's spiciest food. Sichuan hotpot is the province's best-known dish, consisting of a large pot of boiling water that sits over a flame on your table into which the diner throws a host of food, ranging from strips of beef, pieces of chicken, to exotic mushrooms local to the region. The city is also famous as the site of a strangely populist mayor, Bo Xilai, who from 2007 to 2012 fostered a revival of Maoism, including singing old "red" Maoist songs. He became the champion of a movement known as China's New Left. He was dismissed from his post in 2012 following a scandal involving the death of a British citizen who had worked for him.

In 2015, I visited a suburb of Chongqing called Changshou, a small city with a population of 800,000, about 80 kilometers northeast of Chongqing. Most of the buildings were ramshackle although I did spot a Maserati parked in one garage—probably purchased by a corrupt local official. The reason for my visit was to accompany an American fund manager to the heartland of China to get a handle on the country's booming property market. There was a lot of nervousness about the endless property construction in China and whether this would lead to a financial collapse similar to what the USA had undergone just a few years earlier.

But there was a bigger question that I had been grappling with for some time. If, indeed, China's property boom was going to bust, how were China's thousands of small cities going to survive? As we touched upon in the Introduction to this book, China's semi-Federalist system meant that local governments are heavily responsible for their own finances. These local regions are not truly Federalist—they have no real political autonomy from Beijing and have to respond to Party orders from the center—but they have a great deal of *financial* responsibility for everything from health care to government revenue; 70 percent of expenditure on social services is under their purview.

The gasoline that had fueled their fast-paced growth for more than a decade was a combination of land sales and Shadow Banking. Could they keep this up? We had heard that some of the worst problems of China's drunken binge of construction occurred near Chongqing, mainly because the formerly powerful Bo Xilai had the political clout to commandeer significant amounts of capital to plunge into the building boom.

We hired a car for the 90-minute trip to the outskirts of Chongqing, passing through miles of rolling hills, dotted with animals and greenery, the further out we ventured. There was little economic activity and none of the hulking industrial plants a visitor finds in Northeast China. In fact, it looked almost pastoral, as if we were Wisconsin farmers on the way to the market to sell cheese.

Eventually, we passed a Changshou Government Centre that was in beat-up condition and clearly little used. Changshou is an economic development zone approved by the State Council in Beijing and officially is the center of the chemical industry featuring companies like British Petroleum, Sinopec, China National Petroleum, and the German chemical giant BASF. However, we saw few active industries, and I was a little bemused at the description of the importance of these companies to the region's growth, given how little evidence there was.

After passing through a winding road through town, we ended up at the other end, and suddenly the construction we heard so much about was in front of us. As far as the eye could see were hundreds of high-rise residential buildings. I counted some 200 of them, each about 25 stories tall, with a half dozen apartments or more on each floor. No one was around. There were hardly any cars at the base of any of the buildings, nor people walking around, or lights or any other sign of activity. What was going on?

Clearly, this was an example of a classic property boom driven by a drunken credit binge. Why also would there be so many empty apartments? While there was no official data about new residential capacity in Changshou, we compiled our own figures. We estimated there were 200 residential buildings, each 25 stories, with 10 apartments per floor, about 80 square meters per apartment. These are rough guesses but give us a ballpark figure. This amounted to 4 million square meters of new residential construction, or 20 square meters for every family in Changshou. It is highly unlikely that all the families, or even many of them, had enough cash to buy a spanking new apartment, and judging by the fact that it was so quiet you could practically hear a pin drop, most of them were empty.

To understand the importance of property to China's Shadow Banking boom, we must first look at how China's fiscal system works.

***

In 2015, the investment bank Goldman Sachs asked my firm to collect data on revenue among local governments in China. China was about to allow local governments issue bonds on a massive scale for the first time and nobody could figure out how stable these governments were. Did they have a strong fiscal position or were they on the verge of bankruptcy?

What myself and my team in China quickly found is that it is almost an impossible task. There was plenty of fiscal data on China's provinces. However, beyond China's 31 provinces, major regions, and special large municipalities are smaller units. These are another 284 cities, 2,854 districts, 40,466 towns, and 900,000 villages. I swallowed hard and did the best I could to paint a picture of local government revenue.

While from afar it looks like Beijing is in charge of the country's economy, in fact much of the income and expenditure is controlled further down the political hierarchy. This feature of China is crucial to understanding the growth of Shadow Banking. As we will show later, Shadow Banking ended up bridging the fiscal gap between Beijing and the provinces.

The central government in Beijing consists of the premier and the State Council, which includes all the departmental heads, 35 members in all, who make key decisions. The State Council meets every six months. In between, the important Standing Committee makes interim decisions. The Standing Committee consists of the premier, one executive vice premier, three vice premiers, and five state councilors. They, along with the Communist Party, with its tentacles spread throughout the country, wield tremendous power.

But that's not the whole story. Below the leadership in Beijing sit a number of governmental entities that control a large portion of the Chinese fiscal purse. In fact, China is very much like the USA in one important way: a fiscal Federalist structure. Similar to American states, local governments in China are responsible for a significant portion of taxes and social welfare expenses. China's fiscal system is among the most decentralized in the world. More than 70 percent of China's public expenditure is made at the sub-national levels, in contrast to the average 19.6 percent in developing countries and 22.3 percent in emerging economies (Shen et al. 2012a, b).

The central government is responsible for national defense, economic development including universities, industrial policy, and administration of national institutions. Sub-national governments are in charge of delivering day-to-day public administration and social services such as primary and secondary education, public safety, health care, social security, and housing. Those are expensive services. The World Bank noted that counties and townships account for 70 percent of education spending and 55–60 percent of health spending. In 2009, the central government accounted for only 18.1 percent of all government spending. Provinces spent 17.3 percent, and the remaining 64.6 percent was the responsibility of the sub-provincial governments (Ministry of Finance 2011).

What does this mean in practice? When it comes to fiscal budgeting, Beijing may set policy guidelines and act the role of policeman, but much of the control—and cost—of fiscal policy occurs lower down in the political hierarchy. Beijing may wield a big stick but the hitting is often left to the hinterlands. Each political group does its best to push fiscal responsibilities down to lower levels while asserting the largest possible claim on revenue.

Much of today's system was engineered by one man: Premier Zhu Rongji. Zhu (pronounced Ju) was one of China's strongest leaders in recent history. He was premier from 1998 to 2003. He was a widely traveled English-speaking technocrat, with a fondness for Peking Opera. Premier Zhu came to office in 1991 under the leadership of Party Secretary Jiang Zemin. It was a time of crisis for China. Prior to their arrival, the heady days of growth under the dynamic Deng Xiaoping unchained China from the political shackles of Mao and had created a free-for-all economy. Deng's reforms were very healthy for economic growth. But there was just one problem: much of the tax revenue from local firms accrued to local governments. All those profits from the new, free-wheeling capitalist firms stayed local. Beijing wasn't getting much of a cut.

As a result, the national government in Beijing was gradually losing control of tax revenue. The central government budget plunged from one-third of GDP in 1978 to a low of 11 percent (Ibid., Challenges of Municipal Finance).

Desperate to restore fiscal order to the ailing state, in 1994 Premier Zhu struck a deal with local governments. They would give back a bigger portion of taxes to Beijing, and in exchange, Beijing would return funds back to them in the form of intergovernmental transfers. A few years later, in 2002, the central government further ordered sub-national governments to give 50 percent of personal and enterprise income tax over to Beijing. It was a great deal—for Beijing. Local governments lost out. Once the tax system was reformed, local governments lost control of much of the revenue.

Since then, the central government has had a healthy fiscal economy, while the rest of the country's governments have struggled to make ends meet. Beijing, which once spent 50 percent of the government budget, by 2011 was only responsible for 17 percent. The remaining expenditures were distributed among the four levels of government: 18 percent at the provincial level, 22 percent at the municipal (or prefectural) level, and 40 percent at the county and township level (Ibid., Challenges of Municipal Finance, p. 281). This fiscal system has made things difficult for local governments.

By the late 1990s, many local governments were behind in their payments for pensions, along with salaries for teachers and civil servants, and many other government services. The rural sector suffered the most since they are at the bottom of the pyramid.

As the International Monetary Fund noted in one report:

> Following the 1994 intergovernmental fiscal reform, the central government's share of total fiscal revenue increased from less than 30 per cent to around 50 per cent in 2012 ....Local governments are now responsible for much of infrastructure investment, service delivery, and social spending, which together account for about 85 per cent of total expenditure. Local governments also have few own revenue resources and little discretion over tax rates and policy, which makes them increasingly reliant on central government transfers. However, these transfers mainly cover current spending, leaving a smaller margin to finance infrastructure spending. (IMF 2014)

As we mentioned in the Introduction, from 1998 to 2011, the gap between local revenue and expenditure totaled 18 trillion renminbi (IMF 2013). This was a giant hole to fill. The situation had become worse over time because China gradually had begun privatizing state firms. That is a good policy in the long run but had the unpleasant effect of dumping a lot of retirees onto the shoulders of local governments. Instead of the steel mill paying employee dental bills and retirement income, the local governments took on that responsibility.

In 2013, my team took a close look at how five different provinces earned revenue. Taxes, which in Western countries are the largest source of public revenue, ranged from a paltry 21 percent of total revenue in poor Ningxia province to 59 percent in the much wealthier Jiangsu province. For those poorer provinces, Beijing tried to step in to provide extra funds. Intergovernmental transfers from Beijing ranged from 16 percent in the wealthier provinces to more than 50 percent in the poorer provinces. But even with larger transfers, shortfalls remained. Clearly, Beijing was not inclined—or didn't have extra funds—for higher transfer payments.

Given this huge gap in revenue, where would the money come from? Some economists have argued that Beijing could have increased transfers back to local governments. However, much of the revenue controlled by Beijing is tied up in defense and foreign affairs. It would be difficult for Beijing to pare expenditure in these key areas.

How is public expenditure distributed in practice? In 2005, total central expenditure was 1,125.55 billion yuan. This was only 24 percent of government spending. The central government allocated most of its financial resources to national defense (21.74 percent of the total central expenditure), servicing the interest on public debt (14.17 percent), and capital construction (12.13 percent). Sub-national government spending was 3,527.30 billion yuan, accounting for 76 percent of total government budgetary expenditure. The most important spending items at the sub-national level included operating expenses for culture, education, science, and health care (15.64 percent of total sub-national spending), operating expenses for education (10.57 percent), and capital construction (7.59 percent). For specific sectors, sub-national governments accounted for 94 percent of the expenses for education, 98 percent of the expenses for health, and 87 percent of social security subsidiary expenses (Shen et al. 2012a, b).

In addition, often the top leaders are not interested in supporting local services. Social welfare isn't necessarily a top priority in Beijing. The key determinant of Beijing expenditure may be political loyalty. As academic Victor Shih of the University of California at San Diego noted, "China does not operate like a federalist democracy. Far from it, the findings (in this paper) reveal that autocratic governments with a long time horizon like China have an incentive to conduct intergovernmental transfers in order to *maintain the loyalty of grassroots officials.*" In other words, transfers are usually not performed for reasons of equity but for distribution of power (Shih et al. 2008).

Under Chinese law, local governments are not permitted to run a deficit, a rule designed to prevent them from accumulating too much debt. Formal tax rates are relatively low and tax collection inefficient. So where did the local governments find additional revenue? Over a period of decades, the local towns turned to what are known as "extra budgetary fees" to fill the gap. These could include everything from garbage disposal to school registration.

However, the largest source of new income for cash-starved local governments were fees from land and property. Fueled by a property boom in the 2000s, and then the fiscal stimulus, property values soared. The deed tax for property became the fourth most productive tax at the prefectural and county levels. Combined with the property tax, the land VAT, and urban land use tax, in one year, 2007, the four taxes levied on land and real estate produced 17 percent of tax revenues at the prefectural level and 16 percent at the county level (Challenges of Municipal Finance, p. 287).

Local governments jumped into the land business with a vengeance. Land sales provided a considerable boost to fiscal revenue. Over time the revenue stream from land increased. Direct taxes from land accounted for about 10 percent of total fiscal revenue. Indirect taxes such as sales and corporate income taxes generated from construction and real estate companies in some cities amounted to over 50 percent of total fiscal revenue—that's a big chunk of income for cash-starved local governments. In some places I have visited, the property market in general accounted for 80 percent of local GDP.

Thus, beginning in the 2000s, land became the financial bedrock for much of China's fiscal system. Land, which once was the source of rice for the country, had become a giant piggy bank for local governments.

As a result, property values kept climbing. Real estate prices in Shanghai, for example, from 2003 to 2011, jumped 150 percent. The story has been the same across the country. Property, along with construction and everything that goes along with it, became a significant generator of economic activity in China. It also turned ordinary peasant land into a gold mine for local governments. They realized they could buy the land cheap—often by force—and sell it to developers for multiples of what they paid for it.

Travel across China anytime after 2005, and particularly in 2010 when the stimulus was in full force, and you would see rows upon rows of high-rise apartment blocks. One city in Inner Mongolia called Ordos even became the poster child of China's giant property bubble. Fueled by soaring commodity prices, the city and local citizens poured money into property construction. As money ran out, it became clear there was no real demand for empty blocks, and the local economy collapsed due to lack of real jobs while buildings sat vacant like a baseball stadium on an off-day.

The Chinese would argue that these huge apartment blocks were necessary to provide new housing for the rising urban middle class, who left farms to move for jobs in the cities. There is a great deal of debate about the size of urban migration. Some argue that the impact of urbanization, although a significant trend over the long-term, is also partly myth. Some urbanization is actually simply a rezoning of rural areas as part of cities. Also, many of the urban migrants are poor laborers, doing service jobs at low wage rates, who cannot afford to buy a nice apartment in a downtown high rise.

At bottom, much of the property bubble was fueled by local governments' hunger for new sources of revenue. Who would complain if the township sold the land to a developer, who banged up a cheap building, and then everyone reported a nice fat addition to GDP to Beijing's number crunchers? By the time the building turned out to be a Potemkin village—which increasingly is what was happening—the officials who created this fabricated village would have moved on to their next post.

This may seem like a long digression, but it is important to understand the backdrop of local government financing to comprehend why Shadow Banking jumped so sharply in 2009. Although there are other causes for the rise of Shadow Banking, including a search for higher income among citizens, and a source of capital for private businesses, local government financing was a huge part of the growth.

***

Changshou was not alone in Sichuan with too much construction. Nationally, the official figures state that land sales account for approximately 40 percent of local government revenue. The GDP contribution nationally is around 30 percent. In Chengdu, according to local analysts, property was 65 percent of GDP at its peak in 2007 but had fallen to 34 percent at the time of our visit in 2015. But we were told it was as high as 80 percent in the rural areas. It certainly looked like Changshou had poured an awful lot of concrete over the past few years. The data for the province as a whole showed significant weakness in the property market—far worse than the official National Bureau of Statistics numbers would suggest. The weakness was apparent even in the capital city, Chengdu, which was healthier than the surrounding regions. The value of land sales in Chengdu, another large city in Sichuan with a population of 4.3 million, had fallen by one-third since the peak in 2010 to an estimated 46.8 billion yuan in 2015. In volume (in Mu or 16 percent of an acre), they had declined by two-thirds since the peak in 2010.

During our visit, local Chengdu property agents said that inside the center city there was a 10-year supply of residential land and a 15-year supply for commercial construction. For all of Chengdu, there may have been as much as a 30-year inventory of land for commercial use. Although there were 2 million square meters of land built or under construction, based on actual permits filed with the city government, there was 140 million square meters of potential build. This is an inventory of approximately 30 years. We spoke to an agent who assisted the government in conducting land transactions. "In 2013, we would beg the government to sell land. Now, the governments come to us. They are desperate to sell land," the agent told us. In 2014, one small city outside of Chengdu was unable to sell any land at all.

Property analysts frequently use a ratio of investment of real estate to fixed asset investment to estimate consumption patterns. This is an important measure because it analyzes infrastructure compared with real estate growth. Fixed asset investment is money spent on physical assets such as roads, bridges, machinery, or property. If the real estate portion is very high, that means that there is too much investment in property compared with productive assets like machinery. The figures below show how high this has become in China—particularly in the smaller cities. In the USA and Europe, real estate generally is less than 10 percent of fixed asset investment. It's much higher in China—a sign of a property bubble.

In 2015, the ratio for Chengdu was at 20 percent, and Chongqing was at 30 percent. For all of China, the ratio is 35–40 percent—basically a bubble—while Sichuan is 30–32 percent. Overall, real estate investment grew rapidly from about 4 percent of GDP in 1997 to 15 percent of GDP in 2014, accounting for 15 percent of fixed asset investment and 15 percent of urban employment. Most of this investment occurred in the smaller cities. In China, the four largest cities (known as Tier I cities) only account for 10 percent of floor space sold. Six Tier II cities, usually provincial capitals, account for nearly 50 percent, and smaller cities

(Tier III/IV) account for more than 40 percent of the floor space sold (Chivakul et al. 2015).

The big question was how was this shell game going on? Who was providing the money? If the property market was overbuilt, as our visit implied, why would the money continue to pour in? We discovered a couple of sources of capital—and many were from Shadow Banks.

In Sichuan province, we were told that Chengdu and surrounding towns were raising money from a number of places. Many of the sources of capital were from Shadow Banks. These inflows came from:

1) **Trusts.** Persuading local Trusts to buy the land. Most Trusts in China are partly owned by provincial governments and are thus under some pressure to support local government initiatives.

2) **Government Investment Company.** The biggest company in Sichuan that has been involved in land purchases during our visit in 2015 was a company called Chuantou Energy, listed in Shanghai. Chuantou's principal business is hydropower generation, but it also is in a wide range of industries including thermal hardware and software and power supplies for mass transit systems. Technically, it is not an LGFV, because it is directly owned by the Sichuan government (LGFVs are legally private companies separate from the government). We can only guess where Chuantou obtains its capital, but given its government ownership, it is likely to have been able to access inexpensive bank loans and raise capital from Shadow Banking sources such as Trusts and WMPs (Wealth Management Products). Because it is owned by the provincial government, it is an easy target when the government is looking to stimulate the economy by selling land.

3) **SOEs.** (State Owned Enterprise) State firms often lease land directly from the government or indirectly through LGFVs. This helps to prop up land values and increase government revenue.

4) **Hospitals.** This was the strangest story we heard. Essentially, Changshou asked local hospitals to vacate downtown land and move to the suburbs, thus freeing valuable land for resale for commercial or residential uses. We were told that the extra cash was used to pay for needed social services such as health care.

5) **Pre-Mortgages.** Increasingly, the local governments are "mortgaging" the land to the bank. This is essentially a pre-sale based on future cash flows. Obviously, it is a risky transaction because land

values are declining so the banks will be left with an asset with declining value. One example of land mortgaging occurred in the Chengdu district Dujiangyan with 60 billion renminbi of local debt. The local government had been required to pay the debt down in 2013 but forced the banks to roll over the loans. To pay off this debt and increase cash flow, it mortgaged future land sales to local banks. Dujiangyan convinced property developer Dalian Wanda to purchase the land for 55 billion renminbi to pay back the mortgage. This is incredibly scary and risky because the government basically is creating a derivative contract based on future land sales—at a time of falling land prices. It's pushing these obligations on to the banks without declaring them as loans.

As we can see, Changshou was relying on a combination of formal loans through the banks and Shadow Loans through the Trusts and other groups.

During our trip, we met with the Chongqing government official who regulates small lenders; these are the mini-Shadow Banks. He said the CBRC (China Banking Regulatory Commission) in 2014 began registering small lenders, removing that responsibility from local governments. In 2015, there were 7,000 private lenders in Chongqing, according to official statistics, with total lending of 60 billion renminbi. They were allowed to charge incredibly high interest rates, as high as four times the official government rate or about 25 percent. That's a big burden to put on a struggling property company and theoretically should have led to a huge number of defaults. However, the official data for NPLs (Non-performing Loans) was quite low—just 0.24 percent in 2014. Local officials said they expected that to jump eightfold, to 1.5–1.6 percent in 2015. Of course, the unofficial rate was probably much higher.

"The small debt companies have NPL rates much higher than what they report," the official said over cups of tea in a local hotel. "As long as interest is paid, they keep extending the loans. The real rate is probably around 5 per cent."

In the end, we left Sichuan almost as confused as when we arrived. There seemed to be no clear pattern of capital flows. It was all being channeled through hidden conduits, like moles burrowing underground, digging hidden caverns of stored grain. Except in this case, it wasn't clear there was any grain.

***

In November 2010, the most vehement bear was probably Jim Chanos. He was featured in a blistering article for Fortune Magazine when he called China "Dubai Times 1000." Chanos' obsession with China began with the commodity boom. As Fortune noted:

> It started in 2009, when he and his team at Kynikos looked at commodity prices and the stocks of big mining companies. "Everything we did in our micro-work [on commodities] kept leading us back to China's property market," Chanos says. China's construction boom was driving demand for nearly every basic material. One day, at a research conference in 2009, Chanos listened to an analyst tick off numbers about the scale of China's building boom. "He said they were building 5 billion square meters of new residential and office space—2.6 billion square meters in new office space alone. (Powell 2010)

I was fortunate to have a private meeting that year with Chanos and his analysts at Kynikos' offices in midtown Manhattan. I had written a note for clients entitled "Is Nanjing an example of a Chanos moment" and sent it to him. He called me in for a meeting. Although he hadn't visited China himself, clearly his analysts had done their homework and had decided that China's property boom was going to turn into a bust. Their analysis was correct although they were a few years too early.

Through many visits to smaller cities in China with the Bank of China International, I, too, had become concerned about the rapid growth of China's property market. Increasingly, I was of the opinion that the problem was mainly due to fiscal constraints on local governments. My belief was that analyzing China's property market using macro data provides only part of the picture. Many of the most pressing issues were really best understood as local issues. How much debt was there, who held it, how much new housing was coming on stream? I realized from my trips that these issues were being hotly debated locally among the three most interested parties: the local government (municipal or city), the local branches of the state banks, and the local arm of the PBOC, the Central Bank. .

I assembled data on one city—Nanjing—to see what it could say about the impact of the property market on the economy and why Shadow Banking had become such an integral piece of the puzzle. It was pretty clear that Nanjing—and many other cities—was spending more than its revenue in the hope that property values would appreciate and the city could use rising land sales to repay their official bank and Shadow Banking loans.

I looked at Nanjing because it is fairly typical, albeit wealthy, with a population of 7 million. It is more tied to the healthy eastern seaboard than some other cities such as Wuhan and Xian, but it is not immune to the issues from the property boom. With my assistants, we assembled total government revenue, including listed land sales.

Fiscal revenue (tax and other receipts) for Nanjing in the first nine months of 2009 was 65 billion renminbi, rising a year later to 79 billion renminbi. Infrastructure investment for the same periods was 195 billion renminbi and 233 billion renminbi. Basically, Nanjing was spending more than double its income on fixed asset investment, of which real estate was a significant portion.

Where was the money coming from? How much of the expenditure was paid by the local government directly, how much was loaned by banks, and how much came from Shadow Banks?

Beijing had offered to pay only for intercity rail. The rest was up to the Nanjing government. We could assume that most of the infrastructure investment was government related, including government buildings, roads, and subways. Some highways were privately funded because they could generate income through tolls. In addition, some infrastructure projects traditionally have been funded by SOEs, such as the giant oil companies, although this investment had been declining. It was fair to assume, though, that most projects, however, were either direct government creations or were quasi-government through LGFVs.

However, much of the property investment is likely to have been privately funded and shouldn't be included on the local balance sheet. So for arguments' sake, we eliminated real estate as a government obligation. That still left 151 billion renminbi and 177 billion renminbi of infrastructure investment for 2009 and 2010, which was more than twice government revenue.

We have left out one important source of revenue excluded from the total that helped to prop up the whole house of cards: revenue from land sales. The official Nanjing data put a fairly modest value of land sale revenue at 3.9 billion renminbi for nine months of 2009 and 10.4 billion renminbi in 2010. Independent company Soufun cited a much higher number, of 45 billion renminbi in 2010. Let's assume Soufun was correct. If we add that back to government revenue, that gets us up to approximately 120 billion renminbi in 2010—still about two-thirds of infrastructure expenditure (ex-property) of 175 billion renminbi. That's an annual shortfall of 50 billion renminbi, about 40 percent of government revenue including land sales.

Where was that extra 50 billion renminbi coming from? A good guess would be Shadow Banking. Trusts, WMPs, and entrusted loans most likely provided a hefty share of the investment during this period and helped fuel the property boom.

The revenue shortfall was probably higher in Nanjing than some cities as there were likely off-balance sheet investments that were not even included in the city data but should be regarded as government debt. In addition, Nanjing is better situated geographically than many cities in China due to its proximity to the wealthier coast.

Clearly, Nanjing's finances were unsustainable. It was in the interest of local governments to keep land prices high to sustain the illusion they could pay off their debt burden in sales of future appreciated land. Over time, though, stricter lending standards, higher interest rates, and tighter rules by the PBOC and CBRC regarding off-balance sheet financing gradually would make it difficult for property to continue to appreciate at this rate. It was clear from our data, though, that Shadow Banking was the glue that was holding Nanjing together.

* * *

Hefei, the capital of Anhui province, is a mild-mannered place without the feel of the overheated boom towns like Beijing. Save for a new development zone on the outskirts, half-built property projects are relatively scarce, nor are there giant stadiums or elaborate light rail transport as found in Chongqing and Xian. With a group of fund managers, I traveled to Hefei to figure out how bad the fiscal situation was and whether the top officials had a handle on it. As we have been arguing throughout this book, Shadow Banking helps serve the state as much as it does private enterprise. But how do we see where that line is? One way is to do a check of local finances.

We paraded into a conference room, three fund managers and myself. Across from us was a phalanx of top Hefei officials. They were there at the invitation of the local branch of the Bank of China, hoping for a big investment from the American contingent. The story they told, though, was not encouraging.

According to the director of the Hefei Finance Office, in 2010 Hefei had tax revenue (ex-land sales) of 47.6 billion renminbi. After remittances to Beijing, revenue was 25.9 billion renminbi, just short of expenditure of 26.7 billion renminbi. In addition, land sales generated another 25.9 billion renminbi of revenue.

GDP had been healthy for the previous five years, at around 10 percent growth per year, the tenth highest in China. The underlying economic base was relatively diversified, with 10 percent from manufacturing, 10 percent from consumer electronics, 10 percent from financials, and the remainder from a variety of other industries. Tax revenue had been rising an average of 35 percent a year over the previous five years.

And, at least at the time, the property market looked a lot less "bubbly" than in many other parts of China. Prices rose 5 percent in 2006, 5 per cent in 2007, and 15 percent in 2008 and 2009 and didn't undergo a big jump until 2010, rising 35 percent. The price of land had risen fourfold, from 1 million renminbi per mu (0.165 of an acre) in 2006 to 4.3 million renminbi per mu in 2010. That increase had been less than the 5–10 times jump in some other cities. Hefei's real estate price increases ranked tenth in the country and its increase in land sales was number 24—relatively benign. Housing accounted for 25 percent of fixed asset investment, in line with many Chinese cities but below a few of the faster growing ones.

All this sounds reasonable—except for one thing: debt. Debt—including Shadow Loans—was the catalyst for the growth. And it was huge.

Hefei had outstanding loans of 436 billion renminbi, a ratio double GDP, which was 270 billion renminbi. This is a much higher ratio than the average US cities, where most are well under 50 percent. Conveniently, city officials lumped all of the debt into a single category, making it impossible to figure out if the debt came from banks or Shadow banks. Debt had risen 30 percent from 2009, which was 40 percent higher than in 2008. Almost one-fifth of the loans were poured into LGFVs.

Despite the avowedly diversified economy, fully 30 percent of fiscal revenue came from the property industry. Add in construction, and property-related GDP was to 50 percent. That signaled bubble territory.

The government hoped to pull a rabbit out of a hat by doubling down on fixed asset investment—but they planned to try to steer it away from property. Total FAI (Fixed Asset Investment) had been running a titanic 400 billion renminbi per year.

Given this debt-fueled investment, no wonder there was a labor shortage in Anhui, a province long known as a source of inexpensive labor for the rest of the country. (Beijing's famous silk market where many tourists buy fake Gucci bags is owned by an Anhui native and many of the shopkeepers are Anhui migrants.)

WHEN IN DOUBT....BUILD A TOWN!

Where was all this money going? One big borrower was a large development zone on the outskirts of the city. It was designed to be a financial center, along with residential and commercial buildings, a giant sculpture, walkway around the city's lake, a high-speed rail terminal, three hospitals, and a school moved from another section of the city. Capacity was to be 16 million square meters of residential space, enough for 300,000 people, nearly 20 percent of the population. Hefei was investing 10 billion renminbi per year, with 4 billion renminbi from the government. The official banks lent the first batch, but the rest would come from Shadow Loans and land sales. Demand for the new district was artificially stimulated by moving many of the banks and central government offices from downtown to the new district. Officials acknowledged this could cause downtown office and residential prices to fall. The government's initial capital was pushing up land prices, thus boosting government revenue, in a virtuous cycle. It wasn't necessarily a Ponzi scheme, but certainly there was a lot of money chasing money to push prices up—and create more money.

Social housing was also a component of growth. Beijing classifies social housing into four categories: public or corporate housing (presumably for state employees), economic housing sold to residents, lower-end public housing for the poor, and corporate housing in general. In 2010, the city built 800,000 square meters of social housing and had plans to add 2 million square meters annually. They assumed this social housing would provide homes to workers who would increase the tax base. This was a suspect concept given that many residents were relatively poor.

Hefei officials displayed a peacock attitude of "exceptionalism" I had witnessed elsewhere in China. Every city in China likes to think it is special. Every city is on the verge of becoming the next Chinese Silicon Valley. Those low-interest loans from the banks and Shadow Banks help to feed city egos. "Hefei is different from other cities," the head of the new development zone said. "Hefei is healthy and outsiders are moving in. We won't see any dip in prices in Hefei." Almost every trip I made to China I would encounter a local official eager to say that his city would be a center for excellence for a certain industry (usually something sexy like technology) and attract upper middle-class residents who would rush to buy property. The problem was, usually just a few kilometers away was another city mayor boasting of a similar plan.

* * *

The fiscal changes in China over the past two decades were a double-edged sword for local governments. On the one hand, they allowed capital from both the formal and informal financial sector to flow into local economic activity, out of sight of the controlling politicians in Beijing. On the other hand, they caused tremendous waste of capital, as local officials took advantage of their fiscal freedom to indulge in spending that contributed little to growth. Separating the wheat from the chaff is the job of financial intermediaries—banks. China's fiscal Federalism created an environment where the wheat and the chaff were thrown into a giant mixer while the farmers (local officials) simply hoped for the best.

China has made great strides in developing its economy and in providing basic sustenance to its people. But the country's fiscal underpinnings have become increasingly shaky. A policy to support Beijing's tax base caused gradual erosion in provincial revenue. China's great real estate boom, encouraged by the fiscal stimulus, kept the local governments from collapsing. Shadow Banking provided much of the capital.

CHAPTER 5

The Rise of the LGFV

Before his luxurious lifestyle came crashing down, Xing Libin was the unofficial mayor of Luliang. He was at bottom a local businessman, but because he became so rich and his companies were so well connected with the government, he became more powerful than the local officials. When I visited Luliang prior to his downfall, I asked local people about Xing Libin. "Oh, he's rich," one said. "There is his own office building." It was like walking into a small town in Texas to discover that the man who owns the gas station is also the police chief, mayor, and principal stakeholder in the local bank. The main difference is that the stakes are not in the millions in China, but in the billions. Liansheng Group was the tenth largest coal company of more than 130 in Shanxi, and the biggest privately owned one, as well as the biggest private company in the province.

At its peak at the end of 2011, Liansheng Energy had total assets of more than 60 billion renminbi and 36,000 employees. It owned 38 mines with total production capacity of 35.5 million tons per year. With more than 4 billion renminbi in personal assets, Xing was one of the top ten richest people in China in 2007 and 2008.

Xing Libin's empire is among the 10,000 companies that were a hybrid between the state and the private sector. Although Xing Libin had listed one of his companies, Shougang Fushan, on the Hong Kong Stock Exchange, Liansheng could be considered an LGFV due to its tight connections with the government.

© The Author(s) 2017   53
A. Collier, *Shadow Banking and the Rise of Capitalism in China*,
DOI 10.1007/978-981-10-2996-7_5

LGFVs can be considered the shock troops of China's stimulus package. They were the ones sent to the front lines to find—or create—"shovel-ready projects." They were wildly successful at spending money—who wouldn't be—but since those heady days have become albatrosses around the neck of the state. They also were among the biggest borrowers of Shadow Loans and are a prime example of how China finds creative ways to twist itself into pretzel shapes to negotiate between the private and the public sector.

While investment companies had operated since the early days of China's economic reform, they flourished following the 2008 stimulus. The LGFVs have close state connections but obtain capital from bank loans and private sources. All told, China has more than 10,000 local, off-balance sheet companies. The National Accounting Office 2013 survey estimated that they accounted for 39 percent of the 17 trillion renminbi in local debt—a figure that has since risen to 24 trillion. This official figure may underestimate the amount of debt they have incurred.

In 2007, each LGFV, on average, borrowed 540 million renminbi through ten loans from 2.3 banks. The LGFVs increased their borrowing dramatically in 2009, almost doubling the number and amount of loans from 2008. The total amount of outstanding loans for LGFVs increased to 7.7 trillion renminbi in 2010 and dropped sharply afterward. This is mainly due to the 4 trillion renminbi stimulus package implemented from November 2008 to December 2010 (Gao et al. 2016).

The first of these companies was established in Shanghai in 1992. Called the General Corporation of Shanghai Municipal General Corporation, it was set up to coordinate construction of municipal infrastructure projects, including water, sewage, roads, and other utilities. It received both municipal funds and the authority to borrow from banks, and by 1994 had 38 billion yuan in assets. As Christine Wong of the University of New South Wales noted, "Over time, the model spread to other municipalities. By the turn of the century, most cities had established LICs (Local Investment Companies), and they came to play an increasingly key role in financing urbanization in many localities" (Wong, Christine. Paying for Urbanization. Cited in Financing Metropolitan Governments in Developing Countries. Edited by Bahl, Linna and Wetzel. Lincoln Institute, 2013. P300). As they became more accepted, their separation from local governments was relaxed, and the local governments began to guarantee bank loans (Wong 2013).

Although a number of them were shuttered in the 1990s under the disciplined hand of Premier Zhu Rongji, they reemerged in the 2000s, until they exploded in size during the 2008 fiscal crisis. Encouraged by the central government to act as funnels for the government's fiscal stimulus, in 2009 they were instrumental in spending 3 trillion renminbi in new credit, and in the first quarter of 2010, they were responsible for 40 percent of new credit nationwide. Numbers grew to nearly 9,000 nationwide, scattered across all regions and localities, at all administrative levels including townships and towns. They took one-third of all new loans issued in 2009 and 40 percent in 2010. In 2009 alone, the LGFVs increased total debt by 3 trillion renminbi to 7.38 trillion. By year end 2010, total debt exceeded 10 trillion renminbi (Wong 2011).

China's government budget law requires local governments to balance their budgets and doesn't allow them to borrow. The central government recently began imposing ceilings on local government borrowing (quota for bond issuance) and, in principle, promised not to bail out local governments.

However, as the amount of money spent rose faster than the ability to find reasonable projects, their economic function became questionable. Much of their debt is unlikely to be repaid. Most of these companies have acted either as conduits for municipal investment in infrastructure—whose benefits are unproven—or speculative ventures designed to take advantage of China's roaring property market, both residential and commercial.

***

Over the years, the LGFVs also became popular because they helped to promote local leaders. The popular belief in the West is that Chinese leaders have a strategic long-term view of politics. In his book, *On China*, Henry Kissinger states that Chinese leaders have a philosophical outlook similar to the Chinese game of "Go." He calls this strategic encirclement. "The balance of forces shifts incrementally with each move as the players implement strategic plans and react to each other's initiatives" (Kissinger 2011).While it is true that there is a lot of back-and-forth in Chinese politics, which we discussed in detail in the chapter on Federalism, many politicians are quite direct in acting in their own self-interest. They are just as concerned about self-preservation as, say, the Mayor of London. They wish to move up the rungs to a higher position, potentially in Beijing itself. Chinese politicians are like politicians everywhere; they are eager to marshal enough support to stay in power and, if lucky, get promoted.

Quickly. That means that ten-year strategic plans are far less important than rapid—and visible—success.

Promotion often is tied to vanity projects—even if they aren't economically viable. A paper by political scientist Victor Shih at the University of California in San Diego argues that local Chinese leaders are not moved up the hierarchy by how well they keep the economy growing. Instead, what really matters are two factors: connections to leaders in Beijing through school, local birthplace, or industry affiliation, and the politician's ability to bring in revenue, a skill long treasured by millennia of Chinese emperors. Revenue doesn't just mean taxes. In fact, for most local governments, property and employment taxes are a small part of the pie. The bigger source of revenue is service fees and the sale of land (Shih et al. 2012).

That's where the LGFVs became a godsend to power-hungry officials. The huge 2009 stimulus, with money flowing like water down a mountain after the snow has melted, was perfectly suited to the dreams of local officials for higher office. They could put the money to work constructing flashy projects and point to them as proof of their political power. And dream they did. Suddenly, glamorous projects multiplied manyfold and became the golden opportunity to prove they had the right stuff for promotion. Repeatedly, leaders came up with sexy-sounding investments, coaxed willing investors to put up some capital, and marketed the heck out of the new project—in time for their next promotion.

The ultimate goal was to move to a new position before the whole house of cards came tumbling down. In fact, in many cases, the peak investment period for a newly appointed Provincial Governor is two years after their appointment—enough time to put in place a sexy project while still allowing two more years to showcase the investment before the next move up the ladder.

***

A trip through the town of Luliang, a booming coal town of 300,000 in China's biggest coal province, Shanxi (pronounced Shan-shee), is a startling reminder of how much modern China looks like an Asian version of the twentieth-century American company town. Like Detroit in its heyday, when the Ford family wielded immense power through the family's automobile company, there are scores of towns across China dominated by local companies and rich entrepreneurs like Xing Libin. The crucial difference between General Motors in Detroit in the 1950s and Luliang before Xing came crashing down is the role of government. During their heyday, the Fords were no doubt given favorable treatment by the Mayor of Detroit. But that relationship pales in comparison to the deep roots between entrepreneurs and governments in China. The blurred line between the state and capitalism was readily apparent in Luliang, embodied in Xing Libin, a private businessman. Along with the local government, Shadow Banking played a major role in his rise to fortune.

Luliang itself is an unprepossessing town, a dusty place sliced through by a river, ringed by mountains slashed by the black lines of dozens of coal mines. Six out of the city's 13 counties are among the country's poorest. Luliang is just 400 miles southwest of Beijing but is a grueling eight-hour drive due to the rough highway. To get there, you need to fly into Shanxi's capital city, Taiyuan, and then take a bumpy three-hour bus ride through rolling hills pitted with coal mines.

As I drove through the town on a brisk spring morning, fighting to breathe through the polluted coal-laden air, the taxi driver kept pointing out evidence of Xing Libin's private company, the Liansheng Group, known as Lasen Energy in English. Next to the river was Libin's private hotel, the Shanxi Liansheng, a spanking new hotel with a giant lobby that senior Communist Party members used for private gatherings. I found this out when I tried to book a room there two days after the conclusion of the Party Congress in Beijing. That's when local officials meet to disseminate the decisions from the top. I discovered that the senior leadership of the Luliang County Government had reserved all the rooms for the two-day gabfest. With two colleagues, we drove up to the hotel and managed to grab an expensive lunch there in a private room on the second-floor dining room, but only after bypassing the guards at the gate and running through a throng of local party apparatchiks, all looking very jolly (perhaps drunk) despite their formal party garb of white shirt and dark suit.

Across the river from the hotel lay the town's tallest structure, naturally called the Liansheng Building, which housed the group's employees. Next door to the office tower was a tall apartment block that was the private Liansheng Group residence, where Libin and his family resided—before their downfall—in a top-floor penthouse. The number of Liansheng Group corporate assets in the town of Luliang boggled the mind.

Xing Libin was a small but important player in the largest coal-producing province in China, which is the biggest coal consumer in the world. China ranks third in coal reserves, behind the USA and Russia, producing more than three billion tons per year. The country has been fighting an internal political battle to reduce its reliance on coal to slow the onslaught of thick yellow pollution that coats the tongue and creates headaches if you stand outside for too long. Coal mining officially kills 2,000 people a year, but the actual number is most likely much higher. There have been some victories in the closure of smaller mines, mainly due to their poor safety record. But, with investment in coal growing 50 percent a year after the financial stimulus, coal was still China's largest source of energy, accounting for 73 percent in 2014.

I traveled to Luliang to investigate Xing Libin more than a year before his empire collapsed. I was looking into the relationship between Xing Libin's private company, Liansheng, and a public company called Shougang Fushan. He was the head of both. Under securities law in most countries, including Hong Kong where his company was officially headquartered, transactions between a public company and one owned by an employee have to be transparent to investors. You can't run a public company while doing business with your own company on the side, unless you reveal the nature of the dealings between the two. There was a suspicion that Xing was profiting from his private company without notifying any shareholders. While there was modest discussion in the official financial filings in Hong Kong about the company and the Liansheng Group, there was a distinct lack of detail about exactly how the transactions between the two functioned.

I encountered first hand the question of the close connections between the state and the private sector in the Xing Libin Empire when I visited one of the local Luliang schools. Xing's public company had stated that it was donating $17 million a year to the local public schools. The company financials noted, "Certain mining companies in Luliang County, including Xingwu, Jinjiazhuang and Zhaiyadi, are obliged to pay subsidies for the improvement of educational infrastructure and facilities in the Luliang County including construction of modern schools and provision of educational facilities" (Shougang Fushan Financial Filing 2013). It looked like this was a company payment to a for-profit school owned by Xing Libin himself. What was the story here?

As we drove through the dusty streets of Luliang, past new but already dusty ceramic three-story homes, and up the long drive to the school complex, I noted the sign: Liansheng School, the name of Xing Libin's own group. This suggested the company donation wasn't going to the town of Luliang but to Libin's own operation. We stopped our car at the gate and made our way to the security guard. Posing as a visiting businessman considering a move to Luliang (pretty farfetched given that no American in his right mind would move to a town with little modern housing and constantly engulfed in a gray smog), we were led upstairs to the director's office. The director, a tall, unctuous man with the demeanor of a used car salesman, was happy to boast of the tight connections between the town and its richest member.

"The school is a joint venture between Liansheng and Luliang," he said. In fact, so close was the relationship that one of the school's building housed a training institution whose students mainly studied accounting, coal operations, and management and go on to work for the Liansheng Group—all trained at the expense of the local taxpayers and the shareholders of the public company.

However, when one financial firm publicized this awkward fact, the company was quick to disavow it.

> The Report alleged that the donations made by the Company for construction of modern schools went to a for-profit school owned by Mr. Xing. The Company wishes to note that this allegation is untrue. The donations were made in accordance with a notice issued by the Luliang People's Government of Shanxi province to numerous coal producers in Luliang. The donations were directly paid to the Luliang People's Government. Official receipts had been issued by the Luliang People's Government in respect of the donations made by the Company. The Company considers that the making of donations is a way to contribute to the community. (Shougang Fushan Financial Notice)

Technically the company may have been correct. They could have given the money to the local government. But in the end it ended up in the hands of the school. During our travels in Luliang and its larger nearby town, we heard rumors of the real reason for Libin's generosity to Luliang schools. By donating money to the school district, Libin had cut an unofficial deal with the government. In exchange for creating a new institution, including construction a large high school, he would be repaid through reduced taxes. However, we couldn't prove this.

Apart from the school visit, I spent days sitting in cars outside of Xing's coalfields, counting trucks to verify production, picking coal off the ground to test quality, and interviewing locals about what they knew about Xing Libin's empire. It was tiring work. At night, I slept in a hotel room with a television with nothing but Chinese channels. The switch on the wall that said "hot" and "cold" produced neither. The hotel only accepted cash probably because it was cheating on its taxes.

Despite my personal plight, the broader issue that was clear during my visit was the lack of distinction in many towns in China between the public and the private sphere. Entrepreneurs like Xing can flourish in China because they start capitalist businesses but play the Communist Party card when necessary.

An expose´ by the influential Caixin Magazine in Beijing (pronounced Sigh Shin) reported widespread bribery by Xing Libin that went deep into the bowels of the Communist Party:

> As collusion between business and official spread in Luliang, fraud became common in official appointments. In June 2009, Luliang, on the orders of Nie Chunyu, secretary general of the province's party standing committee (and the top official), announced a plan to select the heads of its 13 counties. Strict election procedures were announced. But a local official said that the procedure "looked fair, but without outside supervision, there was actually room for fraud in every stage. Indeed, a candidate who described himself as a vice county head later posted an article online saying he spent 4 million yuan to get a more senior job, but lost to someone who spent more. The author of the post said his funds to buy votes came in part from companies. He said that Luliang was one of the places in China where such fraud was worst. Li Yi, a former Luliang official and a subordinate of Nie's, said the heads of the city's counties and districts usually got gifts worth 50,000 yuan to 100,000 yuan from one individual lower-level official every year before the Lunar New Year holiday. Some got 5 million yuan in total. Those who refused to send gifts would not get promotions, Li said. (Yuan 2014)

Underneath this rotten empire, the glue that held this unruly deal together was Shadow Banking.

The coal industry sucked down a huge amount of Shadow Banking loans. In 2013, of the 11.7 trillion renminbi of money raised by Trust companies, one-quarter, or 2.9 trillion renminbi, was invested in infrastructure, mining, and energy. Xing Libin and his Liansheng Group were beneficiaries of the wash of Shadow Banking funds. The Liansheng Group borrowed 3 billion renminbi from a Trust that led to the company's downfall when coal prices collapsed, which was part of a larger debt of nearly 30 billion renminbi. The good times started to end in 2013 when the coal market entered a downturn as the economy slowed. The average price of coal fell to 200–300 yuan per ton, almost half of that seen in the peak 2008–2010 period. That year, the Luliang city government said its fiscal revenue was 16.4 billion renminbi, down about by half from 2012.

Lenders to Liansheng included the formal banks such as Bank of Communications, China Merchants Bank, Huaxia Bank, and the Shenzhen Development Bank, both state and private financial institutions. On the Shadow Banking side, lenders included Liulin credit unions and a host of Trusts. Beijing Trust was owed 50 million renminbi, Shanxi Trust 1 billion renminbi, and Jilin Trust 10 million renminbi. Remember, the Trusts were collecting private company and personal funds and funneling the money to entrepreneurs like Xing Libin.

Xing Libin was detained at Shanxi's Taiyuan airport in March 2014. But his high-level contacts had begun unraveling before then. His detention came right after an investigation of someone much higher up the food chain: Jin Daoming, former vice chairman of the provincial legislature's standing committee. Jin was one of the highest officials in Shanxi to have been placed under investigation by the Communist Party's corruption agency in Beijing, the Central Commission for Discipline Inspection (CCDI). Jin, along with seven vice provincial-level officials, was accused of graft (Caixin Magazine 2014).

Some of them had close career ties with Luliang, according to Caixin's research. In June, the CCDI announced investigations into Du Shanxue, the vice provincial governor who was the party head of Luliang from March to November 2011. In August, Nie Chunyu, secretary general of the province's party standing committee, was put under investigation. Nie spent eight years in Luliang, heading the local party committee from 2003 to 2011. Shortly after Nie's fall, an inquiry was launched into Bai Yun, a member of the provincial party standing committee. Bai served on the Luliang party committee between June 2003 and February 2006.

More officials and businessmen with links to Luliang were investigated, putting the city under a shadow just after the coal industry had made many people very wealthy. The corruption between local Luliang officials and Xing had been occurring since earlier in the decade. In a bid to improve the firm's performance, in 2002 the county decided to hold a public auction to sell part of state-owned Xingwu Mining Co. to outside investors. Official document shows that Xingwu Mining had total assets of 262 million renminbi and 193 million renminbi in liabilities. The company held reserves of 120 million tons of high-quality coal.

Xing won the bid. A local official close to him recalled that he was determined to prevail because "the coal market will get better and better."

But the deal was controversial. Some critics said Xing's offer of 57 million renminbi was far lower than Xingwu Mining's value, meaning a loss for the state on the sale. Others noted that Xing's company was the weakest bidder. An employee of Xing's Liansheng Energy Co., which was established after the deal, said Xing took over Xingwu Mining's debts while paying an extra 10 million renminbi to settle employee claims and another 11 million renminbi for land.

"The assessors of the bidding included 40 local party and government officials, and 39 of them voted for Xing," the employee said (Caixin Magazine, Ibid.).

Once the company was underway, Xing kept the revolving door swinging between his company and the government. In 2009, former Liulin County head Yan Guoping, who led the transfer of Xingwu Mining, became the legal representative for Shanxi Resources Liansheng Investment Co., a joint venture between Liansheng Energy and state-owned China Resources Power Holdings Co. Zou Zhongjia, the former deputy head of Liulin County who oversaw the coal industry, also left government and joined a property company in Sanya, in the southern province of Hainan, that had a close business relationship with Xing. Meanwhile, the chief of Liulin's coal bureau, Ma Xuegeng, later joined Liansheng Energy and became its vice president and vice chairman.

The details about these officials are important because they exemplify the revolving door between the private sector and the state—fueled in this and in many other cases mainly by Shadow Loans. Because Xing was so well connected, the official banks, and the Shadow lenders, believed he could pay them back. After all, his firm included some of the most senior people in Shanxi province, which at the time was raking in revenue from the coal industry.

In addition, China's financial system in general has few systems in place to track credit. There are embryonic credit rating agencies, but most of them are beholden to their corporate customers, and none of them examine the unofficial credit flows among the Shadow Banks. In China, loans frequently are based on reputation and what the bankers call "asset-based lending." This means the banks don't look at the company's revenue or profits but examine what the company owns and whether they have high-level government support. At one point, Liansheng's coal mines were considered a good asset because coal prices were high. And clearly, his government connections were strong.

Who would come to the rescue of all these banks? This is where the weeds of Shadow Banking become entwined with the roots of the State. It's a messy jungle that Beijing will have difficulty untangling.

***

About 30 minutes south of the large city of Nanjing in central China is a small theme park called the Jangling "One Thousand Tree Farm." It is set on 2000 acres of rolling hills and is a farm built expressly for busy city folk to spend the day enjoying nature as an escape from the oppressiveness of Chinese cities. The Tree Farm was an example of the excesses of Shadow Banking in China.

I had heard about the place while investigating the collapse of Shadow Banking loans. There was a report that one loan for 3 billion yuan ($450 million) had gone bust. I was curious where the money had gone and why the project had failed.

The loan had been made by one of the country's biggest source of Shadow Banking loans, a Trust. These are the government-backed institutions that collect funds from individuals and companies for investment in specific projects—basically banks with few regulations. In the case of the "One Thousand Tree Farm," the loan was granted by one of the larger Trusts in China, COFCO Trust, headquartered in Beijing. COFCO Trust is mainly owned by the COFCO Group, a secretive holding company that controls much of China's food-processing business. Although COFCO Trust is a government-controlled company, in 2012 it sold a 19 percent stake to the American financial firm, BMO Financial Services Group. So, it is one of those Chinese institutions that straddle state and private control.

The loan that COFCO organized for the Tree Farm was named the "Finance Jiacheng Real Estate Fund No. 1 Collective Trust Plan." For some inexplicable reason, the Chinese love to label their financial deals with elaborate names. The loan was made to a local government-funded company called Kunshan Chungao. Where had all this Shadow Banking money gone?

On a hot September day, I flew into the capital city of Jiangsu province, Nanjing, famous for vicious fighting that occurred between the Chinese and Japanese in World War II. Nanjing is considered one of China's more pleasant cities due to a tree-planting campaign by Mao's wife after the revolution in 1949. After checking into my hotel, which had a charming outdoor garden facing Nanjing Square, I jumped into a taxi and gave him the address for the Tree Farm. After fighting the honking horns of Nanjing's numerous cars, we finally made our way to the expressway and soon were buzzing out of the city at more than 100 kilometers per hour. We passed waves of fields, dotted with construction sites before exiting the highway to a small, four-lane road.

The cab driver had to ask directions several times before we finally pulled up to the site. Ringed by an eight-feet tall wire fence, the front gate was locked. A guard listlessly walked out of his hut. He told us the place was closed, so we got back into the taxi and drove around the site, and discovered a back road with an open gate. As we drove over a dirt road through the back entrance, we were faced with a series of pools separated by dirt dikes, each containing fish specially grown, placed in the pools to please the urban fisherman. Further along was an area dedicated to fruit trees. Beyond the fruit arbor was a small group of restaurants designed in faux rustic log style. The only thing missing in this beatific scene were customers. During our visit, we saw no tourists or visitors of any kind, and barely a hint of workers, apart from a group of women, eating rice out of bowls, gamely manning one of the smaller restaurants. The leader of the group, hunched over her food, told us the place had been shuttered for several months. "It's a private company," she said proudly.

Why would anyone think they could succeed with an eco-tourism site? It was a relatively remote area from Nanjing to be considered parkland, and clearly, given the lack of attraction, there had not been many visitors from elsewhere.

The answer to this question explains much about how China works and how untrammeled capital can act for good—and for bad. The Shadow Banking system has allowed many private enterprises—and quasi-private companies—to obtain seed capital otherwise unavailable through the traditional banking system. Equally, though, it has encouraged wasteful spending on projects like this eco-tourism site. The "Jiangning One Thousand Tree Farm" is a prime example of capitalism gone wild—and the excesses of Shadow Banking in China. The point of Shadow Banking is to allow capital to escape the rigid controls and political needs of the Chinese state. However, that also means that this capital usually is not well monitored. Projects get off the ground that shouldn't be allowed to exist.

In the case of the Tree Farm, a host of private entrepreneurs, local government officials, and Shadow Banks worked together to create a fancy project whose underlying economic fundamentals were weak. There was collusion between Shadow Loans and a good story. One Thousand Tree Farm is in Jiangning District, in the foothills of Jiangsu province. The farm itself is "a national agricultural tourism demonstration site, an ecological farm, providing a tourism, leisure, farming experience, science training, fitness and entertainment," according to the official literature. In fact, because it calls itself a form of "Agribusiness," its investment was supported by the national Ministry of Agriculture in Beijing—very high backing indeed. The farm also aligned itself with goals outlined by the provincial Jiangsu government. Provinces are only one level below Beijing. Due to their relatively strong political power, the provinces are able to obtain capital unavailable to lower levels in the political hierarchy. The Tree Farm was wisely set up in an official "economic zone" promoted by the province. Established in 1992, the Jiangning economic zone was designed to foster the expansion of the capital, Nanjing, to the southeast. In 1997, Beijing's National Scientific Commission designated the region as a formal "high-tech industrial park," giving it more power. Moreover, its political clout was enhanced when the high-speed railway between Shanghai and Beijing was constructed to run through Jiangning. When the founders of the Thousand Tree Farm were looking for a location to convince investors they had a surefire winner, they couldn't have had a better one than Jiangning. Designing the farm as an "eco-travel" experience solidified it as part of the scientific and economic development zone being encouraged at the highest levels of the provincial and central governments.

But as our visit demonstrated, as with many local projects encouraged by rampant spending, the story never lived up to its promise and it collapsed under the weight of its debts. It was another casualty of the excesses of Shadow Banking.

***

As the stimulus package took hold, the collusion between local governments and Shadow Loans we witnessed with the "One Thousand Tree Farm" flourished across China. Companies found new opportunities to work hand-in-hand with the local governments and LGFVs to tap into the deluge of cash that was pouring through the economy. One curious example of this was China Vast, which was able to convince foreign investors to buy into its shares when it listed on the Hong Kong Stock Exchange. It is worth discussing this because, unlike many of these hybrid public/private corporations, China Vast is a listed company and has published financial accounts.

China Vast was established in 1995 to market land and provide other services to local governments. But the amount of money it collected appeared to be vastly disproportionate to the services it provided. China Vast signed profitable contracts with townships in Langfang, Hebei province, just south of Beijing, and in Chuzhou, Anhui province, four hours west of Shanghai. China Vast said it was different from an ordinary property developer. In fact, it was not a property developer but a marketing machine. China Vast "provides additional services on planning, design, marketing and operation of industrial town projects over a long contracted term" and earns profits based on the "sale of land use rights." What does that mean?

- Planning and design "is conducted by our planning and design department in collaboration with architecture firms and town planning experts."
- Land use consists of "clearing and leveling the land, and building infrastructure such as road, tap water, rainwater, waste water, electricity, gas, heat, communication facilities and television cables." All of this is outsourced to contractors.
- Consulting services include "business registration, project administrative approval, environment assessment and application of permits and licenses, and coordination with third parties to provide property management, cleaning and landscaping services."
- Marketing consists of "promoting the sale of such land converted by us to potential enterprises and attract them to set up businesses." (China Vast Industrial Corp., Offering Prospectus, Hong Kong. August 13, 2014)

But it didn't really do any of this. Instead, it outsourced all of these services, acting as a general contractor. It earned most of its fees from two, relatively small local governments in Langfang and Chuzhou. And the interesting thing about its business model is that it didn't get paid to bring in fresh capital; nor were the size of its fees dependent on any services that it performed. Instead, it *was paid the minute the local government sold the land*. It's a pretty sweet deal to have a business that earns income before any work has been performed.

How much was it paid? These two small towns, from 2011 to 2013, paid China Vast profits of $325 million. In their best year, China Vast made $134 million just from "fee income from sales of land development."

That's a lot of money just to market land. In fact, the company says the bulk of its revenue came from one source: fees for the sale of land in Longhe Park, a 28 million square meter development in the town of Langfang, in Hebei province. And those fees were substantial. From 2011, the company had received $384 million in fees—just for helping to sell land in Langfang. That is $100 in fees from every person in Langfang, which has a population of 3.85 million. Clearly there had been a lot of money to be made from the huge pipe of capital flowing to local governments. Even better, in 2014 China Vast convinced Hong Kong and overseas investors to buy additional shares when it went public. In a sense, foreign investors became participants in China's stimulus program.

But along with the public's money from the share sale, and traditional bank loans, China Vast also tapped the Shadow Banking market. It arranged to receive three different Trust loans, for 928 million renminbi, or nearly one-quarter of its total loans of 3.48 billion renminbi. It had quite a complicated capital structure with money from overseas, Chinese banks, and a host of private lenders through the Trusts.

Apart from China Vast, we found another example of collusion between the local government and an LGFV that appeared to be blatantly fraudulent. This story did not involve Shadow Loans (so far as we know) but shows the financial games that local officials play to convince lenders to supply capital for projects that are often quite shady.

In 2012, the Guangzhou government, the capital of Guangdong province, was considering investing in several construction projects. These included public rental housing, a river restoration project, and investments in roads, a pipeline, and a sewage system. These projects would require about 1 billion renminbi in capital. Guangzhou had the option to finance these with a bank loan. However, bank loans were expensive. If the city borrowed 1 billion renminbi for a seven-year loan, the interest rate would have been around 6.55 percent. The officials were concerned interest payments would be too high.

The city hired a local Guangdong investment banking firm to analyze its options. The securities firm had significant experience helping local governments raise capital through LGFV bonds.

The securities firm first advised injecting local government land into the platform company. As collateral, the local government transferred 11 tracts of land comprising 1.7 million square meters, with an estimated value of 370 billion renminbi. This provided the balance sheet for the shell company.

Before issuing the bonds, a problem arose with the shell company's credit rating. The credit rating agency was willing to give the platform company a "AA−" rating for a seven-year 1 billion renminbi bond, resulting in a coupon rate of 7.44 percent or more. This was even higher than the bank loan. To lower the rate, the securities firm brought in a guarantee company to back the bond, boosting the rating to "AA+" and a coupon rate of 6.40 renminbi.

However, the city officials still weren't satisfied; they were looking for even cheaper capital. So, the securities firm *artificially increased the value of the land and property*. The bank achieved this by using optimistic growth projections and backdated these projections to the land's valuation in 2009, 2010, and 2011. As a result of this accounting trick, the assets were marked up 13 percent in value in 2009, 11 percent in 2010, and 11.5 percent in 2011, according to former employees.

Because of the tight relationship between the local city officials and the auditing company, the financial statements passed the audit. In the end, the shell received its coveted "AA+" rating and reduced its coupon to 6.55 percent.

In March 2013, the local government received the approval from the National Development and Reform Commission to issue the bond. In the end, 900 million renminbi of the bond was sold by the securities firm, while the remaining 100 million renminbi of the bond was sold on the Shanghai Stock Exchange. This is an example of how local governments could continue to obtain money from national sources through false pretenses by working hand-in-glove with the LGFV. Shadow Loans frequently play a part in these deals.

***

The site visits provided some detail on where the Shadow Loans were invested. But to take a broader look, we collected data on 22 LGFVs. Our goal was to understand the investment target and the source of capital. The purpose was to evaluate the potential for risk.

Many analysts examining the details of Shadow Banking focus on companies that issue bonds. In our pool, some of these LGFVs issued tradable bonds but most did not. This is a crucial distinction, as most of the official analysis of LGFVs relies on those that issue bonds, which creates a bias toward the financially healthier LGFVs. For example, the widely used Chinese database, called Wind, has information on 374 LGFVs. But they are the only ones that have issued bonds and therefore have publicly available financial statements. We can't argue that our small subset is necessarily representative but it does avoid this bias.

According to this sample, more than half of the investments were made in the property sector. This appeared relatively small until we examined the next largest category, infrastructure, at 32 percent. Many of these so-called infrastructure projects were likely primarily real estate. Often local governments will bury a property project into an infrastructure investment to make it look more palatable to senior PBOC officials concerned about a property bubble. General construction accounted for the remainder. Others indicate a higher proportion of real estate.

More interesting was the source of capital for these hybrid companies. LGFVs that issued public bonds accounted for only four of 22. Most of the remaining capital was evenly split between bank loans and Trusts products.

In 2010, China's National Accounting Office (NAO) conducted a survey of local debt, much of which was incurred by the LGFVs. Their survey said 80 percent of debt was from bank loans, 7 percent from bonds, and 13 percent from private sources. A 2013 audit from the same agency examined 223 local government financing vehicles, 1249 institutions backed by local government funding, 903 government agencies and departments, and more than 22,000 projects. The audit found that the 36 governments had taken on debt totaling 3.85 trillion renminbi as of the end of 2012, up 12.9 percent from the end of 2010. The survey said bank loans were 56.6 percent and "other" loans were 434 percent. These last numbers imply that almost half of local debt was from the Shadow Banks, which is essentially private money.

These projects were called "private." Their capital often came from private sources, and they were run separately from the government. Was there a government contribution in the form of land? Were some loans funneled from the state-owned banks? Sure. But the politicians could also point to the private loans and the hoped-for profits as benefiting growth.

Is this capitalism? Not really—but it certainly is not the same as state-led investment.

In the survey of China, "China's Great Economic Transformation," the authors of a chapter on China's financial system point to the importance of alternate forms of financing that contributed to the growth of a "hybrid" economy—partly private and partly state-owned. "These mechanisms of financing and governance have supported the growth of a 'hybrid sector' of non state, non-listed firms with various types of ownership structures" (Allen et al. 2009). Shadow Banking has been at the heart of this hybrid sector.

However, over time, these funny LGFV companies became a ticking time bomb. Usually, they had no real economic purpose. Once the capital was collected, and the project was launched, actual profits became less important. Meanwhile, because their ownership was never made clear, no one was really in a position to take responsibility. Who really controls the One Thousand Tree Farm? Is it a government project? Is it private as the woman in the cafeteria said? If the debt goes unpaid, who is responsible? The vast amount of money from Shadow Banking has helped to create this confused economic mess of companies.

Clearly, though, the LGFVs were an important clue to why China's economy kept speeding along while the rest of the world slowed down. It was *countercyclical* spending—basically a Keynesian stimulus. According to one IMF report, LGFV spending helped to increase China's fiscal deficit by around 10 percent of GDP. This helps explain why, despite the significant global headwinds, China was still able to grow by around 9 percent in 2009. By 2011, the deficit had been reduced by around 8 percent of GDP from its peak. In 2012, in response to sluggish activity in the first part of the year, the augmented fiscal deficit increased by around 4 percent of GDP relative to 2011, which helped support activity in 2012 (Zhang and Barnett 2014).

***

However, some analysts believe the waste from these local projects has been huge. Jonathon Anderson, a former economist with the IMF in Beijing, attempted to put a number on waste in local investment (Anderson 2014). He tracked three key indicators over time: reported construction activity (e.g., floor space), steel and cement usage, and, finally, completion of property projects. These three indicators moved in harmony from 2000 until 2007; in other words, developers began projects, used steel and cement, and the numbers reported by Beijing for completed projects matched the consumption of steel and cement. Then something odd happened. In 2008, reported floor space under construction started to climb...and climb...and climb. Meanwhile, property completions and consumption of steel and cement stayed relatively flat. What happened that year? As he noted:

LGFVs, developers and construction entities have been borrowing in droves, they've reported project starts in droves, they report rising construction activity in droves, all of which fits perfectly with the rapid increase in overall credit/GDP ... but there hasn't been any corresponding rise in steel demand, or cement, or electricity or any other input related to construction. There's been no corresponding increase in the pace of final completions.

Basically, it doesn't look like developers were really spending the money.

He also spotted another odd statistic: bank deposits continued to climb. They rose particularly sharply for one category newly created by the central bank called non-fiscal government organizations and agencies, which was designed to capture data on the bank deposits controlled by the LGFVs. These deposits jumped from 6 percent to 30 percent of GDP—in just half a decade. Since there really was no good explanation for these soaring non-governmental deposits, he arrives at only one conclusion: local governments were *stealing* the money. He concludes:

> Think about it. Again, every local government wakes up one morning in 2009 and finds that the central authorities have lifted every single form of credit restriction in the economy. Localities are being entreated—even begged—to lever up and find ways to spend on social housing, infrastructure and urban redevelopment in order to counter the effects of the collapsing global economy and the recently flagging property sector at home. And the preferred vehicles for doing all of this are off-budget, non-official commercial entities that are completely opaque: no regular reporting or statistical coverage, completely beholden to the provincial, city and county officials who oversee them ... and maybe once every couple of years an auditor might show up to see what's going on.

What would you do? Given the incentive structure in China, of course you would borrow and take on projects on a grand scale, reporting the maximum possible amount of activity underway in order to show progress. But with no one watching the till, it would be awfully hard to resist the temptation to side-track the funds, squirrel them away in related official accounts, or pay them out through padded contracts to other connected suppliers and friends, who themselves then hide the money in deposits as well.

How much money may have been stolen by local officials? According to Anderson, as much as $1 trillion, much of this from Shadow Banks. Ironically, this massive stealing—if true—may have had its positive side.

Much of the supposed construction in China may not have occurred at all, so as the property bubble deflates there will be less of a comedown. On the other hand, it is daunting to think that local government officials can get away with such a massive reallocation of funds.

This complicated dance of capital between the different arms of government, the banks, the Shadow Banks, and the people down on the ground spending the money is difficult to describe and to analyze. But it is precisely this dance that tells the story of the unusual relationship between the state and the private sector in China. It is not a straight line. There is no automatic and clear way of separating the state and the private activity in China. It is more of a zigzag. Understanding Shadow Banking is one way of tracing the trajectory of this zigzag.

CHAPTER 6

Don't Trust the Trusts

Despite my fluent mandarin, I had no idea what the Shanghai official was saying. It is rare that I am completely flummoxed during a meeting in China—but this was one of those times. I had arranged a series of interviews with local officials in Shanghai for a group of American portfolio managers who wished to take the pulse of China's economy. This was 2012, a boom year for China's economy—but this group had inklings that the boom was not going to last. The only way to find out was to chat with as many people as possible in the thick of China's economy.

We were sitting in the upscale lobby of a Shangri-la Hotel in the newly built financial area of Shanghai called Pudong (Pooh Dong). More than a decade earlier, I had tramped over to Pudong with my eight-year-old son in tow, and it was nothing but dirt fields and the concrete shells of embryonic buildings, placed haphazardly like broken monuments in a graveyard. That day, my son and I hopped on a creakily old ferry, as locals gaped at the unusual site of a Western father and son, for the sluggish return trip across the Huangpu River to downtown Shanghai. By 2012, Pudong had morphed into a modern urban sprawl containing China's tallest building, the Shanghai Tower, and other huge skyscrapers, along with a giant shopping mall, an Apple Store, and an outdoor elevated walkway that circles the entire central Pudong area. The ferry had been replaced by a modern tunnel choked with Mercedes Benzes and Audis. The headquarters of many European and American advertising firms and multinationals are in Shanghai. The raw newness of Shanghai is shocking to a foreigner because

© The Author(s) 2017
A. Collier, *Shadow Banking and the Rise of Capitalism in China*,
DOI 10.1007/978-981-10-2996-7_6

it struts its cosmopolitan urbanity like a rich kid in a fashionable shopping mall. Once, sitting in a spicy Sichuan restaurant in Shanghai's elegant French Concession district, I was able to order, in English, a Chocolatini (a martini with chocolate!).

At the time of the interview in the Shangri-la Hotel, the man who was causing us so much confusion was the head of research for a firm called Zhonghai Trust. We had never heard of Zhonghai Trust. He tried to explain what it did but the explanation made no sense. It sounded like a bank—but didn't have any depositors. It was owned by an oil company but wasn't in the oil business. What was it?

After a while of this back-and-forth questions, it dawned on us that Zhonghai Trust was one of the largest financial institutions in China—one we had never heard of.

Zhonghai Trust is actually part of one of China's giant oil companies, China National Offshore Oil (CNOOC), a multi-billion dollar state-owned firm that controls much of China's oil industry. At the time, this struck us as a bit of an oddball, something a well-heeled state firm could do to establish with its spare cash. But Zhonghai Trust, we discovered, functions a lot more like a bank than an oil company, with more than 300 billion renminbi of capital. It was big.

What we didn't know at the time is that Zhonghai and other Trusts had exploded out of nowhere to become among China's largest collection of Shadow Banks. Trusts had morphed from the wallflowers of finance into the table centerpiece. But this is how things worked in China. When there is an opportunity or a problem, China will find a way to make it happen. And the Trusts were making Shadow Banking happen—big time.

***

As with many elements of China's Shadow Banking market, Trusts are a uniquely Chinese invention. They are a combination of commercial bank, government piggy bank, and investment fund. To survive, and even flourish, they have acted like chameleons able to adapt to their surroundings, depending on which government agency or company has shone a spotlight on them. At times, they act like a typical bank, making loans. At other points, they function like a retirement fund, convincing Chinese citizens to park their money for long-term capital gains. And frequently, they function as an arm of the local government, making investments according to the whims of the Party officials. How did these weird hybrids rise from bit players in the world of finance to become 12 trillion yuan challengers to China's state banks?

The first Trust—initially called Trust and Investment Companies (TICs)—was China International Trust and Investment Corporation (Citic). It was launched in 1979 as a way for the central government to encourage free markets—while pretending it wasn't really abandoning the Communist system. This was a typical Chinese solution. China likes to experiment to see what will succeed and what will fail, what will gain approval among the widest political audience, and what will sink like a stone. When Deng Xiaoping came to power in 1979 after the disastrous and economically stifling Cultural Revolution, he was desperate to allow the markets to succeed in order to increase incomes of the impoverished Chinese people. He made many steps in that direction, including pushing through the immensely popular and hugely successful policy allowing local rural farmers to start their own small businesses. This, alone, helped generate during the 1980s one of China's longest periods of high growth. Although they've never been the epitome of free market advocates, the Trusts have been at the heart of the tension between state and private control of the Chinese economy.

Citic, the first guinea pig Trust, was created by one of the post-Mao period's richest, and best connected, entrepreneurs. Rong Yiren, who later was widely known as the "Red Capitalist," came from a wealthy family in the heartland of China near Shanghai. Before the 1949 revolution, his father put him in charge of 24 family's textile mills. When Mao took power in 1949, Rong Yiren was one of the few significant capitalists who refused to leave. Although he "was like an ant on a hot pan," in his words, this commitment to the New China gave him significant political currency that eventually led to his rise in 1957 as vice mayor of Shanghai. The sophisticated Yiren, educated at the elite St. John's University in Shanghai, thrived in China in the years directly after the revolution.

But it was his appointment in 1978 as economic advisor to Deng Xiaoping when Deng was promoting a market economy that sealed Rong's position as the leading pro-market individual in China. One of his first acts was to set up Citic. According to Citic's own literature, in the early days, Citic "was a key window on China for both foreign and domestic investment, and a pioneer in Chinese overseas investment" (www.citic.com/ AboutUs/History). But this bloated language obscured the real purpose: Citic would carve out its own little world as an aggressive investor, Western style, within the confines of the Chinese political system, often using for-

eign capital. It would have one foot in the state, through state capital and
state control, and one foot in the markets. This is a classic Chinese strategy. If the rules forbid a particular action, create a new entity to achieve
your goals, but give it a name vague enough to allow freedom within the
confines of the political system. That's one reason many people are confused about the role of Trusts in China—Trusts were never designed to be
a single thing. Instead, they were intended to be a vehicle for investment
in whatever strategic direction the managers decided.

Even though Citic technically was an arm of the state, Yiren ran it as
his private fiefdom, investing in telecommunications, railway, and property. Particularly, Citic cashed in on the growth of China's new Special
Economic Zones. These zones offered reduced taxes and looser regulations to foreign and domestic investors willing to brave the new world
of a quasi-capitalist China. They were Deng Xiaoping's way of injecting
Western capitalism into the strait-jacketed Chinese economy without
overthrowing the fundamental political and economic system. Citic took
advantage of these zones.

Other cities and provinces took note of Citic's growth. They realized that Trusts could be created to invest in their pet projects. While
there are significant budgetary constraints on local and city governments,
Trusts could bypass many of these rules by combining the best of private
and state regulations. They could act like a state-owned company and
utilize state resources, particularly the increasingly valuable land. At the
same time, they could function as private entrepreneurs by going to the
banks to borrow money for projects, which the governments were not
allowed to do. While putting on the face of the free markets, they could
also tell the banks they were risk-free because…voila!…they were owned
by governments! This was clearly circular logic, but it worked under the
peculiar rules of Chinese Communism. According to a report by the
World Bank:

> The original activity of TICs was concentrated in 'the agency business',
> where the TIC acted as a financial fiduciary, taking entrusted deposits
> from institutional sources, for non–discretionary loans and investments
> at the direction of the client. Thus the TIC received a commission but
> bore no credit risk. A large part of the deposits made at TICs have also
> been trust deposits, from which the TICs could make discretionary loans
> and investments, and in this respect its activities, on the lending side, were
> essentially the same as a bank. TICs could engage in financial leasing, store

property, issue securities on behalf of customers, guarantee debts, offer
advice and issue their own securities. Many today trade in securities as brokers on behalf of clients and many are also dealers on their own account.
(Kumar et al. 1997)

This dry description fails to capture the protean nature of these institutions. They could mutate from one financial guise to another like a cuttle-
fish changing colors to evade predators.

To extend the ocean metaphor, the Trusts grew like algae during the
freewheeling days of the 1980s, eventually reaching a peak of 1,000 in
1988. They rose in tandem with the economic freedoms promulgated
by Deng, who was eager to kickstart an economy that was virtually on its
knees. Their growth was supported by the State Council in its "Interim
rules on Promoting Economic Coalition" of 1980, which encouraged
banks to run their own Trust businesses. Citic was among the largest of
these. Apart from its role as a middleman between the state and the private
sector, it functioned as a "window" company. This was a new institution
for China—an investment firm that allowed foreign investors to put cash
to work in China which they initially weren't allowed to do on their own.
Citic eventually became a giant, listed holding company with its own bank
and securities firm. The majority of the early Trusts were founded and
owned either by banks or by Provincial governments, eager to jumpstart
their local economies but lacking the financial resources to do much in the
way of investment.

But there were troubles ahead for these hybrid organizations. By the
end of 1982, there were already more than 620 Trusts, of which 92 percent
were operated by banks and the rest belonged to local governments. Often
the banks were locally owned, too. After a series of scandals, the numbers
fell back to 329 in 1999. The reason for the decline was simple: one of the
country's biggest Trusts went belly up.

In the 1990s, Guangdong International Trust and Investment Company
(GITIC) was one of the highest flying Trusts. Like many Trusts, it was
partly owned by the a provincial government, in this case Guangdong.
For this reason, it was seen as fail-safe. Investors assumed it could not go
bankrupt. So GITIC set out to attract as much foreign capital as it could.
It acted as the fundraising arm of the Guangzhou government through a
controlling stake. It helped to finance projects such as the toll road from
Guangzhou to Hong Kong. Over ten years, it raised billions of dollars to
invest in real estate, hotels, securities trading, and even silk manufacturing.

Unfortunately, GITIC, as with many other Trusts established during these go-go years, was misused by local officials to buy expensive cars, real estate, and other corrupt goods such as jewelry.

After accumulating $4.3 billion in debt, the Japanese and Korean banks that had lent much of this money called in their loans—but GITIC could not pay. It was technically in default. What happened next was the big surprise. The strong-willed Premier Zhu Rongji, eager to shut down rogue investments and take control of China's finances, told investors Beijing would not back GITIC. He officially declared Trusts private firms.

Creditors eventually received only a fraction of their capital—12.5 percent on their investments in GITIC and 11.5 percent to 28 percent for its main subsidiaries. This event in 1998 was a pivotal moment for China's relations with foreign banks and a defining period for China's burgeoning private sector. It was also a key moment for China's emerging Shadow Banks. Zhu had drawn a line in the sand between the state and private capital. Investors were shocked. GITIC had sucked in huge amounts of Western capital with the understanding that it was supported by the government. But it wasn't. Although there were no written guarantees of state control, investors simply assumed governmental support. From then on, foreign investors cast a wary eye on any Chinese institution that claimed it had state backing.

But Trusts weren't dead. They were too useful to local governments. As time went on, they reemerged. The Shanghai AJ Finance Corporation (AJFC) was established in 1986 and approved by the Head Office of the Peoples Bank of China and the State Administration of Exchange Control to engage in Trust deposits and loans as well as the foreign exchange business and other financial services. Organized in the form of a holding company, it was set up by a group of Shanghai businessmen, several of whom had seen their property confiscated in an earlier period. The AJFC had three sources of capital: investment by the owners; deposits, including 80 million in foreign currency; and overseas loans. This Trust eventually mutated into a holding company, with business in trading and real estate, and went public on the domestic Chinese markets. But for a period during the 1990s, the activity of many Trusts was sharply curtailed.

***

The Trusts did not come into their own again until the 2000s. They soon become an integral part of China's Shadow Banking juggernaut.

Trust assets skyrocketed from 3 trillion renminbi in 2007 to more than 12 trillion renminbi in 2012 and a whopping 15.8 billion renminbi by the end of 2015. The number of Trusts remained relatively small—just 68 in total—but they wielded immense power. Just as GITIC became the tool of the Guangzhou government, so did the Trusts become the shovel used by both governments to pour money into their pet projects. Their rapid growth during this period was the direct result of Beijing's 4 trillion renminbi stimulus package.

However, as a result of the freewheeling days leading up to the collapse of GITIC in 1998, the roles of the Trusts changed. Instead of being generalist investors in all asset classes, in the 2000s, they became more focused on local investments. These local investments were a pivotal piece of the larger pie of infrastructure investment to stimulate the economy.

Technically, Trusts are not banks. Nor are they really retirement funds like Fidelity Investments that have custody over funds and invest it as they see fit. They are really just financial brokers. As with most Shadow Banks in China, Trusts take a fee for arranging loans between investors and borrowers. The investors are corporates or individuals.

Nowadays, there are two types of Trusts: collective and single. Collective Trusts are funds gathered from a large number of wealthy individuals, either by the Trust or often in cooperation with a bank, which offers the Trust investment to its wealthy customers. These are actively managed by the Trust—meaning they decide when and where to invest—and generate higher fees of between 1.5 percent and 3.5 percent. In contrast, the Single Trust product is an investment by a single corporation, either state-owned or private, that is seeking a certain level of return and risk. Since there is only one lender and the Trust bears no risk, these generate much lower fees of around 0.01 percent to 0.3 percent. The key point is that *the Trust never has ownership of the money.* It is always acting merely as a dealmaker.

As with much of Shadow Banking, the Trusts took advantage of the uneasy relationship between the state and the private sector. The Trusts have a reputation within China of being owned by the government. This is only partly true. While every Trust is different, 65 percent of the Trusts do have a minority government stake, often by the province. For example, both Yunnan province and Sichuan province have their own provincial Trusts in which the government holds a stake. About 20 percent of the 67 Trusts have an investment by a Beijing government entity, and the remaining 15 percent are wholly private.

Their power is the result of several important factors. First, a license to operate as a Trust is rare, hard to get, and extremely profitable. One PBOC official told me, "The Trusts will never go broke because they can always sell the license. They're quite valuable." Second, their relationship with local provincial and city governments, either through direct ownership or geography, gives them immense political clout. This clout translates into a host of advantages, including a direct line to bank loans, preferential access to investment projects, and, most importantly, a reputation for, dare I say it, trust. Who is going to a question a financial firm with the name Sichuan Trust? Surely the Sichuan provincial government is behind everything the Trust does? Third, the Trusts are an odd state/private hybrid that have slipped through the regulatory cracks because they don't have to follow the same rules, such as loan-to-deposit ratios, as the banks. That's why the Trusts became the go-to institutions when the Beijing government was desperately trying to inject billions into the economy following the 2008 financial crisis.

But acting as both a government and non-government institution is why these oddballs of the Chinese business world have flirted dangerously close to the financial winds. In classic Shadow Banking fashion, they act like private firms to the officials in Beijing, avoiding cumbersome regulations. They don't have to follow rules from the CBRC for risk weightings, or capital adequacy, or most other regulations required of the formal banks. Meanwhile, they are happy to foster the illusion of state ownership when they sell a financial investment to a customer.

In the end, the funds they collect *are not their money*. I am amused when I look at the China Trustee Association website where they have a detailed list of Assets Under Management (AUM). These are not their assets. Unlike Fidelity and other mutual funds, the Trusts are not responsible for the money they collect from investors. They merely collect a fee to arrange a loan.

***

What happens when a Trust product defaults? Who is responsible if these are not their own loans? Given the close relationship between Trusts and governments, it is hard to allow one of these products to fall on its face. There would be too many consequences throughout the political food chain. Officials do not want to be embarrassed or be responsible on their watch for a financial collapse.

One recent example of a failed Trust product definitely caused alarm in the financial world. This was an oddly named financial product called "Credit Equals Gold #1 Trust." In February 2014, newspapers reported that a Trust investment was about to default. The product had been issued three years earlier by China Credit Trust (CCT), one of the country's biggest Trusts. CCT raised 3 billion renminbi for a mining venture, Zhenfu Energy, run by Wang Pingyan, a coal mine operator in the northern province of Shanxi. Mr Wang scaled up his investments dramatically just as coal prices peaked. His company collapsed soon after receiving the loan (Caixin 2014).

The loan was advertised to lenders as offering annual returns of 10 percent and was distributed to wealthy investors by ICBC, China's biggest bank. Banks and Trusts often worked together. It was not the first Trust product to get into trouble: over 20 had reportedly missed interest payments. But Credit Equals Gold promised to be the biggest default so far. As part of the resolution of the debt, China Credit had agreed to sell its shares in Shanxi Zhenfu Energy Group to an unnamed outside party. However, investors were offered repayment of principal but not interest, a loss of more than 200 million renminbi.

Something funny happened shortly after the news hit the Chinese financial press about the ill-fated default: the media went dark. No more was heard for some time about this important collapse in China's Shadow Banking market. It was widely assumed that officials told the press to avoid stories on Zhenfu Energy. These orders could have come from Beijing or the local Shanxi government, whose officials would have been fearful about the repercussions of the flagrant collapse of one of their very own companies that they previously had supported. Since local governments control the all-important publishing license, and most newspapers have Party members on site, no newspaper or television would dare to flout such an order.

Then, the intrepid Western press, in this case the *Financial Times*, broke a story in September 2014 about a deal to save Zhenfu Energy's investors. The story revealed much about how the Chinese financial system operates. The bailout was engineered through Huarong Asset Management (pronounced Wah Wrong), one of four "bad banks" set up in the late 1990s to sell the state banks' non-performing loans. The money presumably came from ICBC bank. This was a highly significant move. The 3 billion renminbi was a private loan to a private company. Huarong, and also ICBC, which distributed the loan, are partly owned by the state. Why should they bail out a local Trust?

Clearly this was a highly sensitive loan because of its size and the involvement of a large state bank, ICBC. To avoid embarrassment to the bank, and ugly opposition from unhappy wealthy investors, someone had to step in to recapitalize the loan. Although Huarong was established to sell ICBC's bad loans when ICBC was selling its shares to list in Hong Kong, it wasn't supposed to continue to bail out the bank once ICBC became a public company. And it certainly had no ties to the China Credit Trust. Yet here it worked with ICBC to recapitalize Zhenfu Energy's bad debt.

This was an example of the blurred lines between the state and the private sector—and how capitalism works in China. A privately owned coal company made a bad decision to expand just as coal prices collapsed. The company borrowed money from private sources—but collected the funds through a government-owned Trust. China Credit Trust investors included a number of private companies, but 33 percent was owned by the state-owned China People's Insurance Group and another 3.4 percent by the China National Coal Group. Still, the loan was a private loan. There was no guarantee by anyone—China Trust or anyone else—that they would repay investors in case of a default. This included Huarong and ICBC. They had no responsibility for this loan and, in fact, weren't really part of the original package. However, it was deemed politically necessary to have an organ of the state step in, and that responsibility somehow fell to ICBC and Huarong. It was highly likely that powerful officials in the Shanxi Provincial Government forced the issue.

In the future, investors would be excused for thinking that any loan by a Trust or any other Shadow Bank was a loan of the State, a promise that would cause endless headaches for all levels of government.

***

The Trusts are among the most dangerous areas of China's Shadow Banking lenders. We will discuss the risks of Trusts and other Shadow lenders in a later chapter, but for now we highlight a few significant risks:

Property More than half of the Trusts that failed were invested in the property business. Over one-third used land as collateral for the investment. Clearly, the property is the most important area to watch when it comes to the Trust industry—as for much of Shadow Banking.

Guarantees Will Be a Problem in the Future Almost three-quarters of the failed Trusts used guarantees to back them in case of default. Among these guarantees, 85 percent were personal and 60 percent were provided by companies. These guarantees no doubt varied tremendously in terms of quality of assets and willingness to provide capital in case of a default. When Trust defaults become widespread—as I expect they will—the amount of litigation and negotiations will strain the regulatory and political system. Even if the defaults don't go to court, the cost of negotiation will consume a lot of political time and energy.

Banks May Increase Trust Ownership Pudong development bank announced in March 2014 that it would acquire Shanghai Trust, becoming the fourth Trust firm under commercial banks following the Bank of Communications International Trust, CCB Trust, and China industrial international Trust. Taikang insurance also bought in SDIC Trust via private placement in January, doubling its capital from 1.8 billion renminbi to 4 billion renminbi.

Banks Will Absorb Losses Single Trusts account for three-quarters of all Trust assets. For much of this capital, the banks were the ultimate lenders, almost 8 trillion yuan in total (for 2013). Assets of the commercial banking sector totaled 125 trillion renminbi at the beginning of 2014. Meanwhile, the amount of single Trust products due in 2014 amounted to 4.1 trillion renminbi. Assuming a non-performing ratio of 5 percent for single Trusts in 2014, a total loss of 0.2 trillion renminbi would trigger an increase by 0.2 percent of the total NPL ratio at the end of the year. The shock at the time of writing was therefore largely absorbable by the banks. However, widespread failures of Trusts would curtail bank loans as they raise capital to absorb the losses. And Trusts are only one part of the bigger picture that is Shadow Banking.

* * *

What does the rise of Trusts in China say about Shadow Banking and Capitalism? As we have discussed previously, Shadow Banking is the use of non-bank financial companies to arbitrage, or evade, restrictions on bank loans and other capital flows. Trusts became a useful conduit to capital flows outside of the formal banking system. But are these flows good for capitalism in China?

The earliest versions of Trusts, the ITICS (International Trust and Investment Company), functioned as arms of the state. They invested in state-approved projects, such as municipal infrastructure, when the government tax and other revenue alone were insufficient to do the job. Over time, they expanded their remit to include a variety of partially private projects and investments. Some of them, such as the Guangdong Investment Trust, used mostly foreign capital to invest in a wide variety of investments. Some of these investments were clearly government (waterworks) and others were speculative and most likely private (property). As *The Economist* magazine noted in 1999:

> ITICs have become the 'treasury arms of local government'. When the returns from pet projects (power stations, toll roads and the like) began to fall, they jumped into ever riskier businesses, gaily sprinkling loan guarantees of their own about, and plunging into share-trading and property development. GITIC, for instance, is the biggest property developer in southern China, with 200 projects and 10m square meters of space. (Economist, January 14, 1999)

These were a hodgepodge of bad investments both public and private.

This burst of activity by the earliest Trusts was quickly shut down by Zhu Rongji, who viewed them as renegade operations. But the later versions in the 2000s became more integral to Provincial financing. Where did they put their money?

Previously, we discussed the role of the LGFVs in Shadow Banking. The LGFVs were a big consumer of Trust and other Shadow Banking loans. How much money did the Trusts give to the LGFVs? According to the 2012 NAO survey, Trusts provided 7.97 percent of total lending to LGFVs. If we apply this ratio to the total local debt of 24 trillion renminbi, then Trusts (or individuals and corporates though the Trusts) supplied almost 2 trillion renminbi to local LGFVs.

We consider LGFVs to be an offshoot of the state because most of them were partially owned by local governments, which tended to favor state-approved projects. But one could argue that their investments in private operations such as property meant that they contributed to the growth of private markets outside of the state system.

Another way to analyze whether the Trusts were providing capital to the private sector is to examine the Trusts' own data. The China Trustee Association provides a breakdown of national Trust investments. For the second quarter of 2015, the largest investments went to corporate loans (22 percent), infrastructure (18 percent), financial firms (15 percent), various financial instruments (22 percent), and real estate (9 percent). The finance industry was no doubt inflated by the stock market bubble that occurred in the middle of 2015.

Unfortunately, for our purposes, there are two problems with this data. First, we don't know the ratio of private to public borrowing among these sectors. For example, corporate loans and real estate, 31 percent of the total, could either be private or public projects. Most were likely going to LGFVs which, as we said earlier, are a halfway house between the state and the private sector.

The other problem is the Trust Association data may not be entirely accurate. The huge growth in Trusts during the 2000s was fueled primarily by the property bubble. The easiest money to be made was to lend to real estate developers. Therefore, the figure of 9 percent Trust assets to property is most likely vastly understated. My own investigation of Trust documents suggests the majority of loans went to the property sector. With my team of analysts in Shanghai, we collected data on 8,524 Trust products for 2010 to mid-2015 and discovered that the median investment in property was 44 percent—far higher than the data provided by the Association. The Trusts didn't want to admit the concentration in this sector because they could incur the wrath of the CBRC. So it is likely the Trusts submit figures to the association that buries real estate loans in other categories such as "infrastructure" and "corporates."

Trusts are likely to remain a significant player in China's financial intermediation. Local governments will continue to use them to invest in local projects—for either social benefit or for pet projects that favor local elites. However, as China makes its financial and economic system more transparent over time, I believe the Trusts will eventually be folded directly into the local government municipal budgets. These governments will use tax money to invest in government-approved projects. This would move China along the path toward a more efficient and transparent fiscal system where there will be little room for cowboy organizations like the Trusts.

CHAPTER 7

The Banks Jump into Shadow Banking

In the summer of 2012, I was sitting in an upscale Japanese restaurant in the pleasant city of Fuzhou on the coast of the East China Sea facing Taiwan, sipping beer with a top executive of a state-owned bank. As he munched on sushi, he complained about the competition his bank faced from the new Shadow Banks, including Trusts and online finance companies. He was worried about how his branch, which was the main headquarters for the entire province of Fujian, would survive against the rising competition from Shadow Banks. The Shadow Banks were starting to eat away at the market share of the big state banks. In retaliation, "We have to begin offering wealth management products or we are going to lose our depositors," he told me.

His comment was a surprising admission of the declining influence of the once all-powerful state banks—and the role played by Shadow Banking. Although many people view China's financial system as a monolith run by a few mandarin officials in Beijing, down in the trenches it's a much more dog-eat-dog universe—and the four state-owned banks are no exception. The comment by the executive was an acknowledgment that the prim and proper state-owned banks had found themselves dragged, like logs down a river, into the muck of Shadow Banking. As the IMF noted:

> Because banks played a major role in financing the expansion, the economic downturn has imposed a significant burden on banks' balance sheets, driving banks to expand off-balance-sheet business, both to circumvent stringent

© The Author(s) 2017   87
A. Collier, *Shadow Banking and the Rise of Capitalism in China*,
DOI 10.1007/978-981-10-2996-7_7

regulation on capital and liquidity, and to tap into new clients and asset classes that are restricted by the current regulation. (Liao et al. 2016b)

But this, in fact, was a journey that had been going on for a long time. From 1950 until 1978, China's financial system consisted of a single bank—the People's Bank of China. The PBOC was both a central bank and a commercial bank. It made all the decisions about lending to state firms. The PBOC broke away from the Ministry of Finance and attained ministerial ranking in 1978 following Deng Xiaoping's explosive political changes. Three other banks were launched to specialize in certain segments of the economy: the Bank of China focused on international trade; the People's Construction Bank of China was devoted to fixed asset investment; and the Agriculture Bank of China was established to handle rural banking (Allen et al. 2009).

But as Deng's reforms took hold, the economy needed more financial institutions than just these four. Over time, a host of private and locally owned banks grew up, including large institutions like China Merchants Bank and Citic Bank, and smaller ones like the Bank of Qingdao and the Bank of Hangzhou.

The banking authority monopolized by the PBOC was gradually broken up. Soon other regulatory bodies sprang up, including the China Securities Regulatory Commission in 1992, the China Insurance Regulatory Commission in 1998, and the China Banking Regulatory Commission in 2003 (Tam 1986). But just as Shadow Banks have to struggle within the context of the State, so, too, formal banks have their power struggles within the financial system.

***

Charles Calomiris and Stephen Haber say in their history of banks, *Fragile by Design*, "A country does not choose its banking system: rather it gets a banking system consistent with the institutions that govern its distribution of political power" (Calomiris and Haber 2014, p. 4). This is certainly true in China. Power flows very differently depending on each bank's place in the Chinese State. The position of the banks is important to understand as we analyze Shadow Banking. Our main point here is that Shadow Banking arose in part because the official banks tended to lend to state firms. They also stood to increase profits through the sale of Shadow products.

The China Banking Regulatory Commission divides China's banks into five categories: the policy banks, the four state banks, the joint-stock or commercial banks, the rural banks, and others, which would include small cooperatives. We look at the banks at one snapshot in time in 2014.

Nearly half of formal credit (not including Shadow credit) flows through the five state banks. The remaining market share is more or less divided between the other groups, with the largest held by commercial "joint-stock" banks, at 18 percent. The chart below classifies the banks according to asset size:

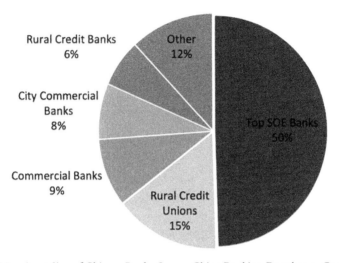

Fig. 7.1   Asset Size of Chinese Banks *Source*: China Banking Regulatory Commission

Our data was derived from the government in the first quarter of 2014. As the competition rose, it is clear during this period that the smaller banks expanded their balance sheets more rapidly than the larger ones. There was a large jump in assets collected in this period to the smaller, non-state institutions. The largest increase in assets came from the city commercial banks, up 22.8 percent, followed by the rural banks, at 16.4 percent. Assets at the state-owned banks rose by less than 1 percent. This was the result of several forces. First, there was excess credit in the financial system due to the monetary stimulus from 2009 and subsequent periods. Second, many of these banks most likely were under pressure from local governments to keep the credit flowing for key projects and to fund property developments that helped fuel GDP growth. Third, they were under pressure to compete with Shadow Banks for depositors and were offering new financial products to attract customers. The same forces applied to the state banks, but they tended to fall under stricter supervision from the PBOC and the CBRC.

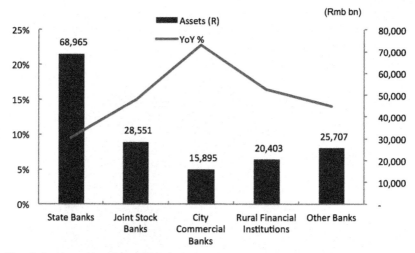

Fig. 7.2   Assets by Type of Bank *Source*: CBRC

Some of the competitive pressures can be unearthed by examining lending patterns. Where did banks lend? The big four state banks accounted for 43 percent of all loans, with the remainder coming from the city, commercial, and rural banks. We can make two quick summary points. First, the banks in general tend to lend to state firms. And second, the banks increasingly engaged in Shadow Lending.

In 2012, approximately one-third of all bank loans—32 percent in 2012—went to state firms. The private sector accounted for another 36 percent, while the remainder went to collective firms (9 percent) and overseas borrowers (7 percent) (Lardy, Markets Over Mao, Kindle Edition, Location 2315). By this calculation, at least half of the money flowing through the banking system ended up in the hands of state-owned firms.

The dominance of state sector loans among formal banks loans was clear during my trips to China. Several years ago, I visited the provincial headquarters of one of the state-owned banks. In the bank's top-floor headquarters, we were served a delicious lunch, including frog ovaries for dessert, a delicacy I had never eaten (one of the fund managers I brought to the lunch texted me under the table … "Do you know what they're serving for dessert? Frogs Eggs!"). After lunch, we visited one of the bank's principal clients, a large energy conglomerate. We had a short meeting with one of the more arrogant chief executives I have met, who clearly felt he was wasting his time. All day the bankers had told us they were careful about vetting their loans, looking at profitability and other financial measures. However, all that careful analysis in the end didn't matter. The client was a state firm owned by the province. It was one of the jewels of the province with arms in a host of businesses in coal, power, building materials, port logistics, real estate, financial services, tourism hotels, and hospitals. As we walked out of the conference room, the banker told me, "We will give them anything they want. They're backed by the government."

But all this state lending isn't terribly profitable for the banks. According to data from the National Bureau of Statistics assembled by Nicholas Lardy of the Peterson Institute, state firms' return on assets reached a peak in 2006 of around 6 percent, just matching the average one-year bank lending rate. Since then it declined fairly steadily, by 2012 dropping below 5 percent—less than the average bank lending rate of over 6 percent.

The private sector, however, had been doing much better. Return on assets in 2012 was close to 14 percent—more than double the average loan rate (Lardy, Ibid., Location 2315). So while the private sector was highly profitable, the state sector wasn't able to generate sufficient profits to pay for the average cost of a loan. Clearly, the state firms were squandering capital.

We can speak more generally (as there is little data) about lending patterns among the other four bank categories. Policy banks obviously lend according to government diktat, be it infrastructure or agriculture or other areas. For example, about half of the new loans made by the China Development Bank traditionally is invested in the nation's infrastructure. But even here there was a fairly frantic effort by the State Council and the Ministry of Finance to push the China Development Bank to invest in the property market—in a clear attempt to support GDP growth (Ru 2015).

***

Data from the rural and cooperative banks is pretty slim, but we assume most of these loans were either for infrastructure or for local government projects or LGFVs. We do have lending numbers from the listing documents for some of the smaller, city banks. Some of the information is worrisome. The Bank of Tianjin notes that its *top ten corporate customers* in 2015 were LGFVs. They loaned them 17.3 billion renminbi or 11.2 percent of corporate loans and 9.3 percent of total loans. That's a significant concentration of the loan book in government-affiliated projects with dubious return prospects.

But many banks' increasingly competitive push for yield led them to invest in dubious areas—outside of their actual loan book. This is regulatory arbitrage, finding ways around the rules for loans by coming up with ingenious new financial products (The US financial crisis, where banks created new mortgage products, is not dissimilar). Why did Tianjin Bank's credit balance to LGFVs rise so quickly? As the CBRC began tracking and restricting loans to local governments, the banks began inventing new ways to circumvent the regulations. These products allowed the banks to provide (or were forced by local governments) capital to desperate local governments. We can only guess why they did this, but it's quite likely the banks were under pressure from local governments to keep the credit flowing. Local credit is extremely important to the local government to support their infrastructure and property projects through the LGFVs, and also to continue to provide capital to purchase land.

Thus, in 2015, the Bank of Tianjin's total credit balance to LGFVs nearly tripled to 52.7 billion renminbi. The credit balance included capital not just in the form of loans but also bond investments (8.4 billion renminbi), Trust Beneficiary Rights, which are loans where the principal or interest is shared with another bank and are considered Shadow Loans (5.3 billion renminbi), and, finally, Asset Management Plans, which are loans disguised as investments (21.6 billion renminbi) (Bank of Tianjin Listing Prospectus, p. 31).

The banks' lust for profits also led them into Shadow Loans. Let's look at one institution—the Agricultural Bank of China. Trust products are funds collected from individuals and corporates that are invested in specific projects. The Ag Bank was collecting money for Shadow Loans to feed the Trusts' ambitious goals. For example, in 2014, the bank's "Interest in Trust Products" rose 45 percent to 248 billion renminbi. The bank was taking a fee for arranging these loans but wasn't keeping them on balance sheet. That's what made them Shadow Loans. Then, the Trust invested them in whatever project they had on their books.

Apart from the sale of Trust products, the Agricultural Bank raised 672 billion renminbi from the sale of Wealth Management Products, an increase of 63 percent from 2013. These are similar to Trusts, but solely from individuals. The bank charged 0.75 percent, making a tidy 5 billion renminbi profit on these WMPs.

***

Another form of Shadow Loans that the banks engaged in were entrusted loans. These are a method for corporates with too much money to lend it out to other firms. The banks acted as the middleman. There was an explosion of this kind of credit following the 2008 fiscal stimulus because the well-connected state firms could access large amounts of bank loans but often didn't have enough projects to justify using the money. The state firms knew that lending this capital was an easy way to boost their profits. They simply borrowed at a low rate—say 4 percent—and loaned it out at a higher rate (say 6 percent or more) and walked away with a nice profit without doing any work. Why would the banks allow their customers to make loans, essentially stealing the banks' business? Generally, the banks have strict lending requirements that prevent them from lending to certain companies, sectors, or geographies. They also have tended to favor state-owned firms over private firms because they believed they would get paid back. Therefore, they were content to earn interest income and banking fees from their top customers, even when they knew the customer would reloan the funds.

Entrusted lending is a unique feature of Shadow Banking in China. The "entrusted loan channel was set up after a 1996 People's Central Bank regulation which prohibited direct lending between non-bank entities, primarily between enterprises but also by government entities" (Deer 2013). During the heyday of Shadow Banking, the entrusted loan business boomed. It became the second largest source of loans after traditional bank lending. The volume of newly originated entrusted loans reached its climax in 2013. In that year, total Shadow Lending was equivalent to nearly 34 percent of total social financing excluding stocks and bonds and the amount of entrusted lending accounted for nearly 49 percent of total Shadow ending. Entrusted loans' share of total bank lending more than tripled from 6.6 percent in 2010 to 22 percent in 2013 (Chen et al. 2016). Clearly, entrusted loans weren't going away.

Interest rates of risky and non-risky entrusted loans

Description	2007–2013	2010–2013
Bank loans	6.16%	6.00%
Non-risky entrusted loans	7.92%	7.71%
Risky entrusted loans	9.22%	9.05%

Source: NBER, Chen et al. (2016)

***

As the banks faced growing competition, along with the gradual marketization of the financial sector, they devised ever-more clever ways of
evading the rising tide of regulations from the CBRC and PBOC. The
authorities were concerned (1) about excessive lending to the property
sector and (2) the risks of non-transparent loans.

In general, loans must abide by rules about the lending target and the
amount of capital set aside for risks. However, other items on the bank
balance sheets could sidestep these rules. In 2015, the banks dreamed up
a new lending scheme. Going by the fancy names Trust Beneficiary Rights
(TBRs) and Directional Asset Management Plans (DAMPs), they basically were loans disguised as something else. TBRs provided an income
stream to the bank without having all the work of keeping a loan on the
balance sheet. The bank sets up a firm to buy loans from a Trust, and then
sells the rights to the income from those loans to the bank. DAMPs were
similar except that a securities firm acted as a middleman between lender
and borrower.

These oddball financial products jumped from nothing until by
the end of 2015 they reached 12.6 trillion renminbi, accounting for
16 percent of banking sector loans. In the first half 2016, these loans
rose by 1.4 trillion renminbi versus 1.2 trillion renminbi for loans.
They were concentrated primarily in the smaller, more aggressive banks,
mainly the joint-stock banks, city commercial banks, and rural lenders
(Bedford 2016).

What is interesting is what happened next. The CBRC caught up with
the banks. In fact, throughout the history of Shadow Banking, Beijing
allows loopholes for a period of time, and then usually institutes regulations that forbid, curtail, or make transparent the Shadow Loans. Due

to the increasing sophistication of China's financial intermediation and markets, the cycle of "creativity" followed by "crackdown" has sped up.

In the case of DAMPs and TBRs, the CBRC launched a broadside in the form of Document 82. This ruling—not announced publicly but transmitted to the banks—shut down this new pseudo loan. Specifically, Document 82:

- Force banks to make provisions for the underlying assets backing the DAMPs and TBRs.
- Require the banks to register these transactions.
- Prevent banks from selling the credit beneficiary rights to their own WMP portfolio. In other words, the banks can't raise private funds through the sale of WMPs to then buy the bank's own DAMPs or TBRs.
- Tighten qualifications for buyers. This meant ordinary individuals couldn't buy these financial products; only qualified institutional investors were allowed.
- Prevent the banks from signing "repurchase" agreements to buy back the assets. This was a system often used by the banks to offload the risks to another entity—usually while the bank inspectors were in town—with the promise to buy them back at a later date. This financial game was particularly helpful in allowing the banks to evade rules on loans to certain industries (all of a sudden the loan temporarily "disappears") along with regulations for loan-to-deposit ratios.

The financial markets reacted favorably to this hard-nosed document from Beijing. According to investment bank J.P. Morgan, the ruling would:

(1) Have minimal impact on the liquidity of the banks.
(2) Reduce the risk of financial contagion by discouraging banks to own each others' bad loans.
(3) Encourage proper provision for bad loans (Lei 2016).

The quick reaction by the CBRC to these new financial products of the banks showed that Beijing was becoming more aggressive about protecting the financial system. The growing "financialization" of the economy, with rising linkages, coupled with the debilitating scenario of the stock market collapse in 2015, had clearly put Beijing on edge. The regulators were finally erecting a stockade around the wild horses of the Shadow Banking market.

* * *

As the CBRC and the PBOC cracked down on banks, trying to prevent them from making off-balance sheet loans for a quick fee, or investing in Trusts, the banks kept finding new, more clever ways to get around the regulations. By 2015 they had started to move capital from loans to another product they called "investments." We can't really call these Shadow Loans because they are a form of financial intermediation handled by the official banking system. And they are kept on the bank balance sheets. However, this clearly was a way for the banks to compete with the Shadow Banks by earning fees from lending into the riskier parts of the economy without running afoul of the regulators. It was a competitive response to Shadow Banking.

During the 2009 4 trillion renminbi stimulus in 2009, Shadow Lending was transmitted by Trusts, investment banks, and commercial banks, through the sale of Trust and WMPs. Although loosely regulated, these Shadow Loans were reported in financial statements by the Trust Association. WMPs initially were tracked by the PBOC, and eventually were listed on bank financial statements. As Shadow Lending grew, officials at the PBOC and the CBRC became concerned about rising debt levels, so they focused their attention on the Trusts and WMPs. The transparency was not perfect, but there was an attempt to provide at least some data.

The investments provided a new source of credit—with few controls. As credit in the economy grew, these investments rose faster than the loan book.

I examined the balance sheets for the Bank of China, ICBC, and China Merchants Bank in the first half of 2015, to understand how the banks are using investments. I was interested in the size of the portfolio and where it was being invested.

For the Bank of China, loans grew only 4.9 percent and accounted for 54.4 percent of total assets. What is striking is the 21.3 percent increase in investments, rising from 17.8 percent of the balance sheet in the first half of 2014 to 20.2 percent in the same period of 2015. In terms of actual capital, loans rose by 405.7 billion renminbi, while investments surpassed this by increasing by 578 billion renminbi to 3.3 trillion renminbi. This is a significant source of capital for the economy from a single bank. As a comparison, this increase in investments was the equivalent of 14 per cent of the 2009 4 trillion renminbi stimulus.

BOC's consolidated financials	1H 2014	% total	1H 2015	% total	YoY %	YoY Rmb Bln
Loans and advances to customers, net	8,294.7	54.4%	8,700.4	53.4%	4.9%	405.7
Investments	2,710.4	17.8%	3,288.4	20.2%	21.3%	578.0
Balances with central banks	2,306.1	15.1%	2,174.5	13.3%	−5.7%	−131.6
Placements with banks/ other financial institutions	1,130.2	7.4%	1,263.5	7.8%	11.8%	133.3
Other assets	809.9	5.3%	871.4	5.4%	7.6%	61.5

Source: Bank financial statements

To understand the assets the bank was purchasing, we looked at a more detailed breakdown. Most of the assets the BOC bought were debt securities, both domestic and foreign. The domestic portion—referred to as listed outside of Hong Kong—was the largest. These domestic instruments account for nearly half of the outstanding balance of funds in the investment balance sheet or 1.4 trillion renminbi out of 3.2 trillion renminbi. The year-over-year increase in domestic purchases was one-third of the total increase in the investment portfolio or 170.5 billion renminbi out of 563 billion renminbi.

The increase in investments included a group of assets classified as "loans and receivables." This category jumped 22 percent to 3.2 trillion renminbi, an increase of 563.1 billion renminbi. About half of the increase was in government bonds. The most startling change was the near doubling of investments in Trusts, from 154 billion renminbi in the first half of 2014 to 335 billion renminbi in the first half of 2015, accounting for 42 percent of the increase in the BOC's investment portfolio. Trusts were happy to grab capital from the banks as fast as they could.

Bank of China's investment portfolio

Financial investments by type	1H 2014	% total	1H 2015	% total	YoY %	YoY Rmb Bln
Debt instruments available for sale						
Listed in Hong Kong	34.7	1.3%	41.7	1.3%	20.2%	7.0
Listed outside Hong Kong	430.4	16.5%	515.9	16.3%	19.9%	85.5
Unlisted	247.1	9.5%	324.4	10.2%	31.3%	77.3
Equity available for sale						
Listed in Hong Kong	4.6	0.2%	5.1	0.2%	10.9%	0.5
Listed outside Hong Kong	0.4	0.0%	0.2	0.0%	−50.0%	−0.2
Unlisted	33.6	1.3%	35.8	1.1%	6.5%	2.2
Debt securities held to maturity						
Listed in Hong Kong	16.4	0.6%	21.6	0.7%	31.7%	5.2
Listed outside Hong Kong	1,229.2	47.2%	1,399.7	44.2%	13.9%	170.5
Unlisted	178.9	6.9%	193.6	6.1%	8.2%	14.7
Financial investments classified as loans and receivables						
Unlisted	430.7	16.5%	630.8	19.9%	46.5%	200.1
Total	**2,605.8**		**3,168.9**		**21.6%**	**563.1**

Source: BOC financial statements

We performed a similar analysis of the financial statements of China Construction Bank, another state-owned bank that has the same regulatory requirements as the Bank of China. Although the magnitude of growth is not as large, there still was a significant increase in the bank's investment portfolio in the first half of 2015. While loans provided the lion's share of the growth in outflowing capital (54 percent), the investment portfolio rose by a substantial 396 billion renminbi or 22.9 percent of total growth in the portfolio.

Income statement analysis

China Construction Bank	1H 2014			1H 2015		
Rmb Bln	Average balance	Interest income	Average interest rate	Average balance	Interest income	Average interest rate
Loans	8,889.2	256.8	5.83%	9,824.3	274.4	5.63%
Investments in debt securities	3,098.4	61.8	4.03%	3,494.4	70.1	4.04%
Deposits with central banks	2,482.6	19.1	1.55%	2,606.4	19.9	1.54%

Income statement analysis

China Construction Bank	1H 2014			1H 2015		
Rmb Bln	*Average balance*	*Interest income*	*Average interest rate*	*Average balance*	*Interest income*	*Average interest rate*
Deposits with non-banks	540.1	12.5	4.66%	729.3	14.6	4.04%
Financial assets held under resale agreements	233.3	6.2	5.40%	321.3	5.3	3.30%
Total interest earning assets	**15,243.6**			**16,975.6**		

Source: CCB financials

Within the portfolio of debt securities, the biggest increase, 8 percent compared with the year earlier, or 98.9 billion renminbi, came from the increased investments in government bonds. However, bank and non-bank bonds came in as a close second, rising 8.3 percent or 85.7 billion renminbi. The entire portfolio going to banks and non-banks in by the first half of 2015 was a whopping 1 trillion renminbi, while the policy banks were recipients of 539 billion renminbi. That's just from CCB, a single bank.

Rmb Bln	1H 2014		1H 2015			
Breakdown in debt securities	*Amount*	*% total*	*Amount*	*% total*	*% YoY*	*YoY Rmb Bln*
Government	1,234.20	35.51%	1,333.10	36.79%	8.0%	98.9
Central bank	188.20	5.41%	160.90	4.44%	−14.5%	−27.3
Policy banks	537.10	15.45%	539.40	14.89%	0.4%	2.3
Banks and non-banks	1,030.90	29.66%	1,116.60	30.82%	8.3%	85.7
Public sector entities	20.00	0.01%	20.00	0.01%	0.0%	–
Other enterprises	485.30	13.96%	472.90	13.05%	−2.6%	−12.4
	3,475.70		**3,623.00**		**4.2%**	**147.30**

Source: CCB financial statements

We see a similar fast-growing trend in ICBC's investments compared to its loans. While first half 2015 loans rose 5.6 percent or 616 billion renminbi, they accounted for just one-third of the overall increase in ICBC's outstanding credit. One-quarter, or 450 billion renminbi, of the 1.8 trillion renminbi increase came from a 21.8 percent rise in investments.

The change in ICBC's assets

ICBC's assets	Dec-13		1H 2014		1H 2015			
(Rmb Bln)	Dec-13	% total	1H 2014	% total	1H 2015	% total	YoY %	YoY Rmb Bln
Total loans and advances to customers	9,922	4117.9%	11,026	4280.7%	11,642	4358.1%	5.6%	616
Corporate loans	7,047	2924.4%	7,613	2955.4%	7,944	2973.6%	4.3%	331
Personal loans	2,728	1132.0%	3,063	1189.3%	3,266	1222.5%	6.6%	202
Discounted bills	148	61.5%	350	136.0%	433	162.0%	23.5%	82
Allowance for loan impairment	241	100.0%	258	100.0%	267	100.0%	3.7%	10
Investments	4,322	1793.8%	4,433	1721.1%	4,883	1827.8%	10.1%	450
Total	18,918		20,610		22,417		8.8%	1,807

Source: ICBC financial statements

However, the composition of ICBC's investments is slightly different from those of the BOC. ICBC's balance sheet shows a significant increase in purchases of unlisted debt securities. These are less transparent and marketable than listed securities and show the bank's appetite for greater risk compared with its competitors.

Why were the banks making these investments? There were three reasons. One was to take advantage of more lax requirements on risk weightings, provisioning, and impairments, allowing greater use of the bank's capital. The risk weightings for investments are 25 percent compared with loans at 100 percent. The higher the risk weighting, the more capital the bank has to set aside to meet international guidelines for its capital adequacy ratio (CAR). Higher-risk assets are subtracted from total assets for purposes of calculating the CAR. Under regulations from the CBRC, corporate loans have a risk weighting of 100 percent. Other assets, however, have a lower risk weighting, which are better for bank profits because instead of setting it aside they can use more of their capital for loans.

According to the CBRC:

– Claims on specific debts issued by asset management companies to purchase state-owned bank non-performing loans have a risk weighting of 0 percent.
– Claims on the central government and the People's Bank of China have a risk weighting of 0 percent.
– Claims on domestic banks have risk weights of 20 percent to 25 percent.
– Claims on off-balance sheet items including revolving credit or securities as collateral have a risk weighting of 50 percent to 100 percent.

The second reason was to evade lending restrictions. At the time, Chinese banks had a maximum limit of 25 percent of their loan book in the property sector. However, there was no such limit on the investment side of the balance sheet. It is likely that the majority of the loans were going to restricted sectors including property, or to favored state firms that had exceeded internal quotas established by the CBRC or the banks themselves.

But the third reason is most relevant to our theme: the banks were facing pressure from the Shadow Banking sector. They needed to increase their returns in order to continue to attract depositors and maintain profitability. We can see this in the profit margins of the products in which they invested.

Although the banks earned higher returns from loans, the margins on loans were falling while those from investments were rising. As one example, we look at the Bank of China. While the highest return was generated by loans, at 5.11 percent, placements with banks and other financial institutions came in second at 3.79 percent, followed by investments, at 3.56 percent. Most important, the return on investments rose 0.05 percent compared with the previous year, while those for loans fell 0.06 percent.

The investments may have generated even higher returns depending on what risk weighting they had and how much additional capital this allowed the banks to lend. In the future, with lending rates gradually being liberalized, the banks knew there would be a growing margin squeeze on loans. Over time, this would make the investment portfolio even more attractive.

BOC's interest income by segment

Interest income	1H 2014		1H 2015	
	Interest income (Rmb B)	Interest rate	Interest income (Rmb B)	Interest rate
Loans	207.8	5.18%	220.7	5.11%
Investments	41.4	3.51%	50.1	3.56%
Balance with central banks	17.4	1.53%	15	1.30%
Due from banks and financial institutions	27.6	4.78%	22.6	3.79%
Total	**294.2**	**4.26%**	**308.4**	**4.12%**

Source: BOC financial statements

We have delved into the murky waters of bank balance sheets not to muddy our story but to explain in financial detail what was going on in the formal banking system during the huge rise in Shadow Banking. We can't prove that the banks were chasing risky products and evading rules because of Shadow Banks, but it certainly looks that way. And the bankers that I spoke to confirmed they were concerned about the new competition from the non-banks.

What did these new channels of bank lending mean for capitalism in China? Were these investments good for private enterprise? It's very hard to prove this one way or another because the banks stopped providing much detail about where the money was going—state or private firms. We can guess that many of the investments were funneled into LGFVs, whose status within the economy depended on the kind of projects they invested in. Also, property may have been the largest recipient of these credit injections, which, although many projects were private, merely fueled an incipient property bubble. Still, the liberalization of credit intermediation within the banks, arguably, has moved the formal financial system closer to an efficient allocation of capital. Why? Because there was a growing liberalization of interest rates. And this is how bankers are supposed to judge loans—by figuring out what companies provide the best returns. Although this trend was weak, it has been a movement in the right direction toward a capitalist economy.

Next, we look more closely at one of the most important forms of Shadow Banking the banks engaged in—WMPs.

CHAPTER 8

The Wild West of Bank Products

To the banks, WMPs were like drugs to a drug dealer. Once they started selling them, the money was too good to ignore.

WMPs have been China's answer to financial repression. China's rising middle class had become increasingly less willing to put its ample savings into low yielding bank accounts for returns of a few percent. However, Beijing's tight control of the financial system had eliminated most other sources of financial gain. The stock market, for example, accounted for only 2 percent of China's total funding. And the market was widely regarded within China as a casino whose returns were dictated by market manipulation and state control. What opportunities were there for savers to increase their income?

WMPs provided the answer. Savers could turn to private intermediaries— Shadow Banks or formal banks—and make a quick return. They offered an escape route for consumers seeking an exit from China's long history of financial repression. For the leaders in Beijing, WMPs were the State's way of allowing investors to raise capital from private sources outside the formal channels of ordinary banking. Private companies unable to obtain funds from the banks found a new source of capital.

But what exactly were these things called WMPs? There is no precise definition of WMPs because they can be invested in virtually anything. In a comprehensive report in 2015, the Reserve Bank of Australia described them this way:

"Chinese WMPs are investment vehicles marketed to retail and corporate investors and sold by both banks and non-bank financial institutions

© The Author(s) 2017
A. Collier, *Shadow Banking and the Rise of Capitalism in China*,
DOI 10.1007/978-981-10-2996-7_8

(NBFIs), sometimes with explicit principal or interest guarantees. They differ from conventional mutual funds in that their returns are fixed and the products have a set maturity (which is usually fairly short). However, WMPs are also distinct from bank deposits in that the funds raised are invested in a range of loans and securities and the returns offered significantly exceed regulated deposit rates (Perry and Weltewitz 2015)."

But the authors also noted that "there is no universally accepted definition of a WMP." That's a more accurate statement. Basically, whatever you could convince the unwitting public to invest in became fair game. On a research trip to Shanghai, I met with a woman who headed up the WMP sales force for Citic Securities, one of China's largest investment banks. It was a big operation and they were doing booming business. Since I said I represented Western investors, over cups of cappuccino in a small coffee shop she quickly fell into sales mode and tried to convince me to buy one of their WMPs. Every time I asked her, "What would I be investing in?," she answered, "What kind of return do you want?" I said it depended on the risk of the investment. Finally, in an irritated voice, she said, "I think it's a bridge in Nanjing." She clearly had no idea where the money was going and didn't care. Multiply that response by thousands and you have an idea of how much money was being shoved at projects with no name. Most of this occurred in "pooled investments" where the money sucked in by the banks was later allocated to various investments. In 2013, the CBRC banned banks from pooling WMP funds, requiring them instead to map WMPs to their investments one-to-one. However, pooled investments are much easier to manage and it's not clear that the banks ever abandoned this practice.

***

Whatever WMPs were, beginning with the financial stimulus they grew very rapidly. They rose from less than 4 trillion renminbi in 2010 to more than 17 trillion renminbi in 2014, and jumped another 57 percent to 23.5 trillion renminbi in 2015. In 2014, the biggest contributors to growth were the joint-stock or commercial banks, whose WMP balance rose 75 percent from 5.7 trillion renminbi to 9.9 trillion renminbi. The SOE (State Owned Enterprise) banks, reflecting greater caution and more controls by the CBRC, increased their WMPs by a slower 53 percent to 8.7

trillion renminbi. Foreign banks started to exit the business; their WMPs fell 27 percent to 290 billion renminbi. In 2013, The top ten financial fund trading banks, occupying 62.27 percent of the financial products market, were the Bank of Communications, China Merchants Bank, the Industrial and Commercial Bank of China (ICBC), Bank of China, China Construction Bank, Shenzhen Development Bank, Agriculture Bank of China, Shanghai Pudong Development Bank, China Minsheng Bank, and the Bank of Beijing (Ibid., Li and Hsu 2013).

But this growth had one significant impact: it threatened the formal banks, even though many of them were selling WMPs. The growth of WMPs may have been the prime reason for the slowdown in the growth in bank deposits. This is hard to prove as there could be a number of reasons why the growth in savings deposits declined during the heyday of credit in the system and the concomitant growth of Shadow Banking. But we think the huge rise in alternative financing products offered in the Shadow Banking market has to be one of the principal causes of the slowdown. Let's look at the data.

First, savings deposits rose steadily from 30.72 trillion renminbi in December 2010, to 51.28 trillion renminbi in December 2014. Clearly, money was still flowing into the banks from private savers.

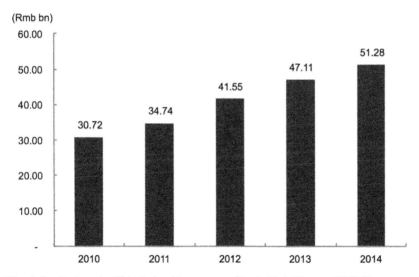

Fig. 8.1   Savings in China's banking system (Rmb Bln) (*Source*: PBOC)

However, the picture changes when we look at the *growth in savings deposits* during this period. The slowdown becomes sharply apparent. After rising in double-digits to a peak of 21 percent in October 2012 compared with the same period in 2011, the increase in savings deposits fell to 8.9 percent by December 2014. Either Chinese citizens had less money available or they were putting it into other investments in the Shadow Banking market, such as WMPs.

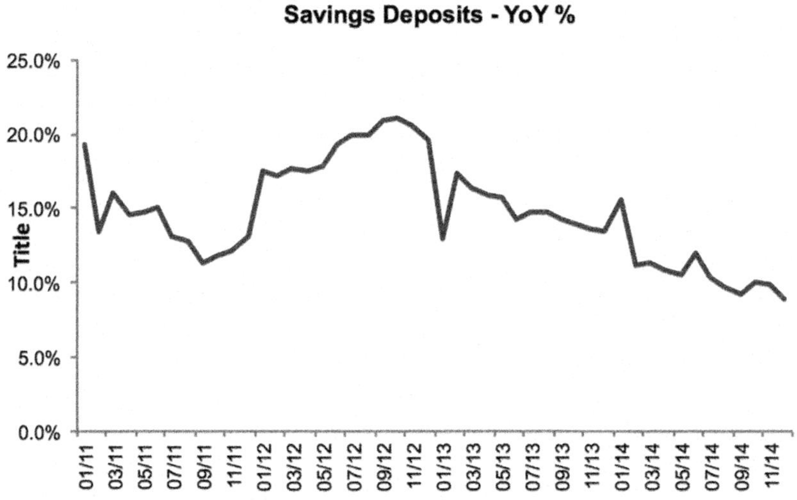

Savings Deposits - YoY %

Fig. 8.2   Savings in China's banking system (YoY %) (*Source*: PBOC)

We think this was mainly due to the WMPs sold by a number of institutions (including the banks) that were invested in a wide variety of investments.

"In fact, horizontal competition from wealth management products is the deciding factor," one senior commercial in Shanghai banker told us. "In order to maintain the current client base, banks chose to launch more wealth management products with higher interest rates, which attracted people to invest by using their deposits."

According to the independent consulting firm CNBenefit, 56,827 Wealth Management Products were issued in 2013, a 75 percent increase compared with 2012. These products raised a whopping 56.43 trillion renminbi, or $8.8 trillion, up 85.9 percent. That was 120 percent of GDP—a lot of cash raised outside of the formal banking system.

THE WILD WEST OF BANK PRODUCTS   109

Apart from institutional and VIP clients, individuals were still the major purchasers, accounting for 72 percent of buyers. By 2013, 40.62 trillion renminbi of personal wealth had flowed into banks' Wealth Management Product accounts. This compares to a stock of total personal demand and saving deposits of only 27 trillion renminbi at the end of the year. The 2 trillion renminbi decline in incremental personal deposits compares with investments of 26.1 trillion renminbi into WMPs.

There is another factor that may have had a significant impact on the growth of WMPs. As we have argued throughout this book, the deposits in the banks are the backbone of the Chinese economy. Financial repression essentially was a means for the state to utilize personal wealth to generate investment for the state-owned economy. This was in effect an implicit tax on Chinese citizens.

But is this tremendous wealth in the banks really savings from the vast majority of Chinese citizens? In fact, we believe that *more than half of the wealth in the banks is controlled by a small group of Chinese citizens numbering approximately 15 million*. If this is true, it has tremendous implications for the Shadow Banking market. If the savings are controlled by the wealthy, then the Shadow Banking loans are mainly their funds—not those of ordinary citizens.

How did we arrive at this conclusion? We looked at the financial prospectuses issued by several local banks in Chinese citizens. Some of them provided a detailed breakdown of the income levels of their customers. We then applied this cohort analysis to Chinese banks as a whole. As a result, we estimate that 1 percent of the population controls more than half of the bank's savings deposits. That's 15 million people with wealth of 28 trillion renminbi ($4.4 trillion).

The implications of this figure—if accurate—are significant for Shadow Banking. This high concentration of wealth would suggest that the majority of private credit that was provided through Shadow Banking channels was actually supplied by a tiny minority of the population. Any default among institutions that borrowed this credit would be restricted to this group. They presumably wield immense political power but, in addition, are relatively concentrated. It's hard to know what the breakdown of this group really is. However, it would be easy to assume that they are well-connected Party members, with ties to the powerful state-owned firms. This means that in any debt workout, the PBOC and the State Council would have to take into account the political power of the elite members of society that loaned trillions of renminbi to jumpstart the economy.

***

The banks weren't the only ones selling WMPs as they grew in size. Others were involved, too. There are three ways to analyze WMPs: by distribution channel, source of capital, and use of funds. Initially, the Trusts were the primary distributors of WMPs. They faced few regulatory constraints and had the contacts to raise the money. Later on, others jumped into the business, including the state-owned banks, the smaller city and rural banks, and even the investment banks such as Citic Securities and China Merchant Securities. As we have noted, the state banks finally joined in. No financial institution wanted to miss out on easy profits. As the IMF said, "In the past five years, wealth management products provided an important vehicle for banks to circumvent the interest rate control, reflecting the increasing role of market forces" (Ibid., Liao (2016c)).

Chinese banks WMPs

	2007	2008	2009	2010	2011	2012	2013	2014
WMP (Rmb T)	0.5	0.8	1.8	3	4.6	7.1	10.2	15
Bank Assets (Rmb T)	52.6	62.4	78.8	95.3	113.3	133.6	151	172.3
Ratio	1.0%	1.3%	2.3%	3.1%	4.1%	5.3%	6.8%	8.7%

Source: IMF

There even arose a type of WMP distributor very similar to the infamous "boiler rooms" in the USA, where hard-nosed salesmen push dodgy stocks on uneducated consumers. I visited one such operation in a small city in China. In a single room, there were several rows of desks, each lined by young salespeople perched in front of a computer screen, busy "dialing for dollars" to convince investors to pony up. The chief executive had thrown up the business less than a year earlier. It's doubtful his young sales force had a clue of what they were selling but were simply offering high returns to unwary customers.

The chart below shows the various channels used to funnel money from wealthy lender to borrower.

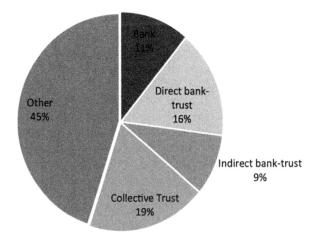

Fig. 8.3 WMPs by distribution channel (2014) (*Source*: Royal Bank of Australia)

As Shadow Banking has grown, all the intermediary financial institutions found ways to work together to collect funds. Sometimes the Trusts worked closely with the banks, or the Trusts collected money on their own, or the banks sold them directly to customers. Their joint activities often were spurred by regulatory obstacles that prevented them from working unilaterally. For example, banks have a large customer base perfectly suited to target sales of WMPs. However, sometimes the CBRC would throw up roadblocks to WMP sales. In response, the banks would turn to the Trusts for WMP distribution, which were not subject to the same regulations.

Banks earn most of their profit from what is called their Net Interest Income (NIM). This is the difference between the cost of the money they borrow (mainly interest payments on savings deposits) and the income earned from lending to companies and other borrowers. In China, this margin accounts for approximately three-quarters of the banks' annual profit. This margin has always been healthy because the PBOC makes sure of it by keeping interest on savings low. (See earlier discussion on financial repression). The remaining one-quarter comes from a host of fees that the banks charge for additional services, such as mortgages, investments, or WMPs. WMPs—and Shadow Banking in general—provided a nice lift to bank profits.

As a reality check, we broke out the earnings for four of the state-owned banks to estimate how much money they were earning from

Shadow Banking. It was sizable. WMP Service Fees accounted for 11.8 percent of fee income in the first half of 2013, 8.7 percent in the first half of 2014, and rose again to 10 percent in 2015. Remember, the banks were really doing nothing more than taking a commission to sell investments to the public. Nice work if you can get it.

Over time, the banks became increasingly eager to enter this business to keep their customers happy and also to generate extra income. I calculated that in 2014 the Big Four state banks earned 50 billion renminbi from the sale of WMPs and Trust products, or a 25 percent of their total fee income, and through the sale of 11.6 trillion renminbi of WMPs. In other words, they raised the equivalent of more than one-quarter of their total deposits of 43 trillion renminbi. They truly were capital-raising machines. What started out as a sideshow soon was operating at the core of China's banking system. WMPs were like a small circus act that became the main event.

SOE bank income from the sale of WMPs

China big four banks—trust and wealth management income (First half 2013)

(RMB Mln)

	Deposits	On and Off BS WMP funds raised	Fees from all agency, trust and WMP activity	Trust, agency and WMP fees as % of total fee income
ICBC	13,580,315	2,811,200	15,243	21.0%
China Construction Bank	11,537,567	3,199,200	11,809	30.6%
Bank of China	7,253,729	2,946,486	10,902	22.5%
Agricultural Bank	10,962,985	2,680,676	12,502	26.3%
	43,334,596	11,637,562	50,456	25.1%
Off BS funds raised		**7,564,415**		

Source: Bank Financial Reports

So why were these Shadow Loans when the banks themselves were selling them? Isn't that just normal banking? This is a tough question to answer definitively because there is widespread disagreement about what constitutes a Shadow Bank and a Shadow Loan. I would argue that what makes the bank WMPs Shadow and not normal loans is that they are off-balance sheet. The bank is technically taking no risk when it markets these financial products (at least legally). This is in stark contrast to a loan, which is the bank's direct responsibility. If it defaults, the bank would have to write it off its balance sheet as a loss. If a WMP defaults, caveat emptor—buyer beware.

Apart from the financial responsibility, a bank loan incurs a series of regulations, including capital requirements, loan categorization, and risk weightings. For most part, WMPs don't have those obligations, although that is changing under the CBRC.

The banks, themselves, complicate the question of financial responsibility (known as Moral Hazard) by using their salespeople and conference rooms to market the WMPs. It's very easy for a salesperson to say something vague like "we stand by these products" even though there ultimately is no bank behind them. Imagine you're an ordinary bank customer and you are told you can double your money. You attend a presentation in China Construction Bank's conference room given by CCB employees. All around you are logos for CCB, one of China's four state-owned banks. Wouldn't you assume CCB was backing the investment?

Breakdown of funds raised for WMP products by major financial institutions	% total
Bonds and money market instruments	34.8%
Structured deposits	32.5%
Loans	21.3%
Bank deposits	4.2%
Other	3.1%
Bills outstanding	4.1%
Breakdown of WMPs by issuer	
ICBC, ABC, BOC, CCB, Bocom	72.4%
Other joint-stock banks	31.0%
Foreign banks	1.7%
Others	1.7%

Source: Bank Financial Statements

Despite efforts by the CBRC to restrict the growth of WMPs, the banks kept on selling them. In fact, they started to cross-invest in other bank WMPs. In 2014, the average bank had 8.8 percent of its assets invested in WMPs. Many had much more at stake. China Merchants Bank had

17.6 percent, or 831.4 billion renminbi of its assets in WMPs. Everbright
Bank was as high as 25 percent.

Bank investments in WMPs

Bank investments in WMPs in 2014					
Rmb Bln	*Assets*	*WMPs*	*Other WMPs*	*Total*	*% of assets*
ICBC	20,609,953	145,636	–	145,636	0.7%
CCB	16,744,130	909,099	–	909,099	5.4%
Ag Bank	15,891,159	672,983	10,613	683,596	4.3%
BOC	15,251,382	846,947	–	846,947	5.6%
CDB	10,317,030	91,502	–	91,502	0.9%
Bocom	6,268,299	NA	–	0	0.0%
CMB	4,731,829	831,473	–	831,473	17.6%
Industrial Bank	4,406,399	628,007	15,413	643,420	14.6%
SPD	4,195,924	575,900	145,874	721,774	17.2%
Citic	4,138,815	376,613	78,859	455,472	11.0%
Minsheng	4,015,136	76,517	–	76,517	1.9%
Everbright	2,737,010	624,457	70,334	694,791	25.4%
Ping An	2,186,459	165,189	64,011	229,200	10.5%
Huaxia	1,851,628	294,619	–	294,619	15.9%
Guangfa	1,648,056	80,647	13,500	94,147	5.7%
Beijing	1,524,437	115,631	–	115,631	7.6%
Shanghai	1,187,452	NA	500	500	0.0%
Jiangsu	1,038,309	76,562	78,079	154,641	14.9%
Evergrowing	848,555	239,543	–	239,543	28.2%
Zheshang	669,957	41,642	80,329	121,971	18.2%
Bohai	667,147	32,132	34,403	66,535	10.0%
Chengdu	634,140	NA	NA	0	0.0%
Median					**8.8%**

Source: UBS

Over a period of time, at the prompting of the CBRC, the banks began
shifting the WMPs to an off-balance sheet position. Technically, they were
no longer responsible for the risk of these assets. The formal change was
apparent in their financials. To take one example, China Construction
Bank's off-balance sheet (non-guaranteed) WMPs rose from 51 percent
of the total in June 2013 to 86 percent by June 2015. The CBRC was
basically telling the banks, "you can keep selling these things but make
sure they're not your problem if they go sour."

China Construction Bank's WMPs

	1H 2013	1H 2014	1H 2015
Guaranteed	489.9	329.5	155.6
Non-guaranteed	526.2	659.4	942.8
Total	1016.1	988.9	1098.4
YoY %	–	−3%	11%

Source: CCB Financial Statements

As we noted earlier, there are significant differences between banks in China. The three major categories are the SOE Banks (China Construction, Bank of China, Industrial and Commercial Bank of China, and Bank of Communications), the so-called joint-stock banks, and the smaller regional banks. They all have different ownership, degree of state control, and reliance on certain geographical sectors and industries. Most important, they have varying incentives to take advantage of regulatory arbitrage in the system.

For Shadow Banking, which would include WMPs, entrusted loans, and other forms of non-bank credit intermediation, the smaller banks often were more desperate than the larger state banks to attract deposits and high caliber borrowers. That's because the SOE banks have the backing of the central government in Beijing and thus are better able to attract higher caliber customers, either borrowers or depositors. The difference in profit motives and incentives means that the smaller banks usually are more aggressive than the larger banks in chasing non-standard forms of credit intermediation; often, this has meant Shadow Banking.

This was clear when three economists analyzed the relationship between monetary growth and deposit growth. The authors note that the smaller banks tended to engage in aggressive regulatory arbitrage more than the larger SOE banks. This occurred during a period of monetary tightening between 2010 and 2013. The tightening caused bank deposits to fall, forcing the banks to reduce lending due to rules governing the Loan-to-Deposit Ratio (LDR). To make up for the decline in profits, they pursued Shadow Banking, in this case by marketing entrusted loans between corporations. Entrusted loans allow corporations to lend to other corporates by using banks as middlemen. The banks do not record this as a formal loan as it is technically not on their balance sheet. As the authors note in their paper on monetary tightening and entrusted lending:

Monetary tightening gave banks a stronger incentive to circumvent these regulations. As the PBC tightened money supply, bank deposits fell. The pressure built up on deposit shortages, which exposed banks to the risk of violating the LDR regulation. Chinese small banks incurred higher costs, implicit or explicit, than large banks to acquire additional deposits when facing random deposit shortfalls. As a result, the LDR and safe-loan regulations, together with institutional asymmetry between large and small banks in coping with un-expected deposit shortfalls, gave small banks an incentive to take advantage of regulatory arbitrage. One effective way for regulatory arbitrage is to increase non-loan investment that was not subject to the LDR and safe-loan regulations and at the same time reduce bank loans that were subject to these two regulations. *Consequently, shadow banking was used by small banks to mask credit risks in the banking system by cleverly circumventing the regulatory restrictions.* (Chen et al. 2016)

The state banks are generally more cautious. They tend to have a stable batch of customers among state and provincial firms and don't need to chase risky profits as much as their smaller brethren. They're also more tightly controlled by both the CBRC and the PBOC, and although they have thousands of branches, they tend to have fairly close links with headquarters in Beijing.

The smaller privatized banks, though, increasingly became the swashbucklers of the banking world, fighting their way into the market like pirates stealing gold. And that meant they were more likely to take on risk. To take one example, China Merchants Bank, one of the larger privatized banks in China, began earning sizable profits from WMP business. In the first half of 2014, the bank earned 4.5 billion renminbi, or a whopping 17 percent of their fee income from this industry. By the first half of 2015, their WMP fees had more than tripled to 11 billion renminbi, or 37 percent of its fee income. In comparison, the state-owned Construction Bank of China proceeded more slowly. Its fees from WMPs (what the bank called Wealth Management Services) rose a more restrained 47 percent to 6.8 billion renminbi, or 10.8 percent of its fee income.

What became even trickier for the banks was what constituted their balance sheet risk and what was simply a transaction that generated a quick buck for the bank. That's the difference between what the banks coyly started calling "guaranteed" and "non-guaranteed" WMPs. The CBRC cracked down on the issuance of guaranteed WMPs and forced the banks to make a clear accounting for them. Still, the ones the banks were responsible for—the guaranteed ones—didn't go away. In the first half of 2015,

China Construction Bank issued 3,355 batches of WMPs, raising a quite significant 2.73 trillion renminbi, or 814 million renminbi per product. By the end of that period, the bank had a balance of 1.098 trillion renminbi, of which the bank was guaranteeing 14 percent.

Clearly, all the banks kept the ball in play in the WMP game because the fees were too attractive to give up. They might receive warnings from the CBRC to stop chasing the ball so aggressively—but they tended to ignore the referees on the sidelines. The spectators (the customers) were enjoying themselves too much, the players were getting rich, and nobody was getting hurt—yet. So why whistle the match to a halt? Charles Prince, the former Chairman of Citigroup was famous for his comment just before the collapse of the subprime market, "As long as the music is playing, you've got to get up and dance." The Chinese banks were dancing.

***

As we will be discussing throughout this book, Shadow Banking is very much a way for Beijing to maintain control of key capital pools while allowing capital to flow outside the formal channels to capitalist and quasi-capitalist destinations. WMPs adhere to this formula. Financial repression encourages—practically forces—savers to find other ways to generate returns. WMPs offered that. Plus, as noted earlier, this money was helping to stimulate the economy, which was one of the top goals for the leadership, particularly during the stressful time during the Great Financial Crisis.

But the risk-reward trade-off of Shadow Banking has been very much in evidence in the market for WMPs. The banks wiped their hands clean the minute the WMP was out the door.

The concentration of wealth in China, which has been steadily increasing, meant that the majority of WMPs were sold to the individual investors. According to the CBRC, at the end of 2015, individual investors, including what are called high net-worth individual investors, accounted for 13.3 trillion renminbi, or 56.6 percent of outstanding WMPs. About one-third, or 30.6 percent, were sold to institutional investors, and another 12.8 percent were sold by banks to other banks. That means that much of the credit propping up China's faltering economy was coming from a small slice of the population.

While the average duration for WMPs in the 2012–2013 period was one to six months, by 2015, buyers were purchasing products that could be instantly redeemed for cash. Buyers, no doubt concerned about the declining economy, refused to make any long-term commitments with their money, preferring to treat their investments in WMPs like a money market with instant withdrawal. The outstanding balance of open WMPs, of which buyers could subscribe or redeem largely at will, rose almost 100 percent, to 10.3 trillion renminbi in 2015. During the year, banks issued 158 trillion renminbi of WMPs, or more than 13 trillion renminbi per month. One American commentator on the Zero Hedge investor website noted that if "WMP buyers decide to 'go on strike' for whatever reason, a liquidity crunch in the shadow banking sector could start quickly." There are no accurate surveys of consumer sentiment in China when it comes to financial products but the declining duration of the purchase of Shadow Banking instruments would suggest gradually falling faith in the economy.

Also, Beijing's overseers sat up and took notice of the growing pool of WMPs and, in particular, the growing risks to small banks. In 2014, the CBRC, the Ministry of Finance, and the PBOC jointly issued, "Notice No. 236: On Strengthening Commercial Banks Deposit Stability Management." The notice banned small banks from acquiring additional deposits through the WMP channel, by offering higher deposit rates (Chen et al. 2016). Then, in May 2015, the CBRC cracked down on another form of investment in WMPs. The CBRC was concerned that banks had created huge pools of "investment products" that were being funded by WMPs. Under the new rules, banks could no longer use wealth management funds to invest directly or indirectly in their own investment products. The lenders would also have to fully provision for the investment products that are based on bank loans (Wildau 2016).

However, Chinese banks are endlessly creative in devising new products. Like a batter stealing bases in baseball, the banks are very good at running to home plate without getting tagged out.

* * *

Have WMPs contributed to the growth of capitalism in China? Yes and no. Clearly, if this huge wave of private capital was allocated efficiently to private enterprises, then the answer is "yes." However, if the money was allocated to non-productive investments stage-managed by LGFVs, or was utilized by firms through "crony capitalism," then the answer leans more toward "no."

One way to assess this is to look at where the WMP funds were invested. In the third quarter of 2015, there were 73,049 WMPs issued, raising a total of 28.85 trillion renminbi. The majority of the funds raised were allocated to a nebulous category, "other." Interest rate products took the second spot, followed by bonds.

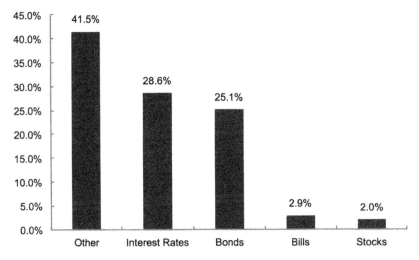

Fig. 8.4 Investment allocation of WMPs (November 2015) (*Source*: CEIC, PBOC)

Note the 41 percent of the 28.85 trillion renminbi, or 11.9 trillion renminbi, that went to the "other" category. While there are many possible investments that could fall within that bucket, the highest returns during the period were probably generated primarily in the property market. (This is not the net figure as there would be redemptions or rolledover credit.)

As we don't completely trust the official figures, in 2013, we also conducted our own survey of WMPs. We were trying to judge (1) where the funds were being invested, and (2) whether they were primarily allocated to pay down debt rather than for new investments. We interviewed sellers of WMPs in 13 cities across China. While the sample size was relatively small, 84 products, we knew the information was accurate because we spoke to the sellers directly.

What we discovered was alarming. First, only half of the money was going to new investments. Fully 36 percent of the money raised was simply to pay down previous debts. The remaining 13 percent was for general working capital. So, almost two-thirds of the money was to fund general operating expenses, and to pay off old loans. Only a small portion was actually devoted to growing the business.

Second, the investments were mainly in two industries: property and infrastructure. These two are frequently mixed together because it suited the needs of private developers and the local government. For example, the developer might build a highway that leads to a property project. I am always skeptical about official data stating that Shadow Banking was invested in infrastructure because the returns are far lower than for other uses.

Within our survey, the remaining 28 percent was invested in financial products and 5 percent in "other" undisclosed investments.

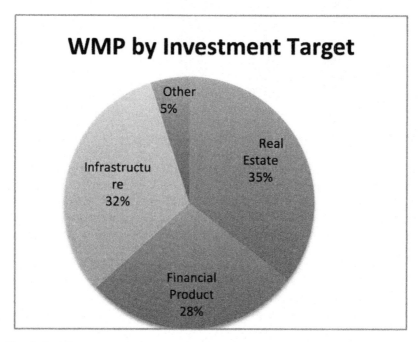

Fig. 8.5 Thirteen city WMP survey (*Source*: Orient Capital Research)

Our interviews disclosed a number of other surprising conclusions. We interviewed more than one dozen lenders and policymakers, including two from the PBOC (Shanghai and Hangzhou) and one from the Bank of China. We were surprised at the general level of cynicism about the inability of the regulators to control local lending. We were told that bankers didn't always pay attention lending controls and found ways to evade them. One SOE banker told us that his bank frequently raised money for LGFVs above the limits set by the CBRC. The bank simply creates a "trust product" as a vehicle for what normally is called a loan. If it is done for a LGFV, the bank then requests the local government to deposit a sum of money equal to the amount of the loan as a kind of collateral, even though it is not labeled as such. Thus, the local government was able to use the local branch of the state banks to explicitly evade lending controls.

Despite concern among policymakers about excess credit from the banks, there was faith among lenders that the economy would be able to bounce back if the stresses became too acute. A banker at the Bank of Wenzhou noted, "Even if there is a problem the (local) government can collect money from other sources, such as taxes or the central government." However, there were companies and banks clearly in trouble, particularly in Wenzhou, known as a stronghold for capitalism and free markets in China. We were told at the time of our interviews in 2013 that losses at the Wenzhou branch of the Shanghai Pudong Bank had reached 50 percent.

The other surprising aspect of the interviews we did for this survey is how little interest there was among the sellers (commercial banks, investment banks, trusts) in the actual investment. Usually, when a bank sells an investment to a customer, there is an explanation of what the customer is buying. (Admittedly, some financial advisors in the USA do play fast and loose with their explanations of the funds they sell.)

In China, instead of asking clients what their "risk profile" was, the banks simply said, "what kind of interest rate do you want?" When pressed, they often could not say where the money would be invested. The assumption seems to be that (1) the lender could create a packaged loan in any size or return, and/or (2) they cared only that there was a government entity somehow related to the product being sold.

This also led to widespread use of loan packaging. This is when a group of investors put money into a fund that invests in a property project. These kinds of investments in the West are generally restricted to wealthy individuals with more than $1 million to invest and there are thick documents explaining the risks. As Shadow Banking boomed, the WMPs had fewer and fewer explanations for where the money was going. This was similar to the slicing and dicing of mortgages by investment banks prior to the

US financial crisis. The intermediaries in China didn't have a clear idea of the underlying projects and were more interested in getting the loans off their books than in explaining them. The banks were having a field day pushing these products out the door and generating huge commissions by doing so. Just like the subprime crisis, where brokers were happy to sell no-money-down mortgages with few questions asked, nobody was forcing the Chinese banks to provide a clear analysis of the risks for the projects they sold. These loans thus were a ticking time bomb.

CHAPTER 9

The Internet Goes Shadow

"The future of finance is the internet," the entrepreneur screamed into the microphone, waving his arms wildly. For the next half an hour, what appeared to be a slightly deranged street performer shouted at the audience about how successful and talented he and his firm were. I was startled. I hadn't seen anything quite so crazy since my time years ago attending rock concerts. Instead of music, though, I was witnessing the "irrational exuberance" of internet finance in China.

In the summer of 2015, I had flown to Beijing to participate in a conference on internet finance. The conference was sponsored by the leading Chinese university in Shadow Banking, the Central University of Finance and Economics, or CUFE. I was one of three Westerners at the conference. My job was to give a short presentation on the risks of internet finance. The other Westerners were two leading scholars of Shadow Banking: Sara Hsu from the State University of New York at New Paltz, and Kellee Tsai of the Hong Kong University of Science and Technology. From the Chinese side were researchers from the two top think tanks, the Chinese Academy for Social Sciences and the powerful Development Research Center for the State Council, and the People's Bank of China. Everything moved along smoothly for most of the day. The mantra was "get money out to the rural folk who are starved of cash"—and online finance was the way to go. It was all very well-meaning.

Late in the afternoon, just as conference exhaustion began to set in, on to the stage leaped the founder of one of the largest online companies

© The Author(s) 2017   123
A. Collier, *Shadow Banking and the Rise of Capitalism in China*,
DOI 10.1007/978-981-10-2996-7_9

in China. After running onstage late to the panel discussion entitled, "Inclusive Financial Service Innovation and Risk Management," he launched into a 45-minute speech—at top volume—about the immense achievements of his firm. He had little data to support his self-praise, but that didn't stop him. We sat in our chairs bemused at his performance, but eventually fatigue set in as we realized he was a classic blowhard (names have been removed for obvious reasons).

That incident made an impression on me. What industry could possibly allow people like him to operate a bank? After all, online finance is nothing more than a giant lending machine—albeit through the internet. Could someone like him really be a key cog in the new world of online financial intermediation?

The answer is yes. Online finance has been heralded in China as the future of finance. As I saw at the conference, it has been endorsed at the highest levels of government. The largest companies in China, including the online transactions firm Alibaba, have jumped into this new market and have been raging successes. Internet finance as a source of capital grew from virtually nothing in 2010 to approximately 440 billion renminbi, or 3 percent of total lending in the economy as reported by the PBOC.

On the flip side, though, online finance is also the Wild West of Shadow Banking. While most Chinese Shadow Banks are on the geographical fringe when it comes to financial flows, the Chinese internet financial firms are practically falling off the map. Until the new internet breed arrived on the scene, most Shadow Banks were part of the existing financial infrastructure. Some were private small-time players, some were partly government owned, others were simply separate units within the Chinese banks.

Internet financial firms were a different game altogether. They sprang out of the woodwork as part of the internet boom. Beijing has been very eager to encourage new industries, and online finance is definitely an important part of the trend. But as they grew, they also have fallen through the cracks in financial system. As we have seen in other areas of Shadow Banking, there is a combination of confusion, regulatory reluctance, and bureaucratic impediments to adequately regulating new forms of financial intermediation. The regulators either don't know enough to formulate rules or can't agree on what to do. This was particularly true for the online world. Imagine you are a serious economist at the PBOC. You have spent your formative years collecting dusty tomes of data about interbank flows or monetary policy. Suddenly, you're asked to regulate an industry that you don't even understand. And you're not sure exactly what the leaders in the State Council think about this new industry—because they probably haven't thought about it. That's why entrepreneurs like the one I saw were able to exist.

Billionaire Guo Guangchang, known as China's Warren Buffett, said the country's fast-growing peer-to-peer lending industry is "basically a scam." Guo, China's 17th richest person with a net worth of $5.6 billion, made the comment in answer to a question at a post-earnings briefing for his conglomerate Fosun. Fosun's Chief Financial Officer Robin Wang had said "we never invested in any P2P projects," until Guo jumped in to add that most peer-to-peer lending was "rogue," according to a report by Bloomberg News (Yang 2016a).

* * *

There have been a number of waves of capital flows outside of the formal banking system since Deng Xiao Ping began liberalizing the Chinese economy in 1979. Online finance is simply the latest iteration of these Shadow Banking channels. Online finance means a lot of different things. It can include purchasing goods on Ebay or Amazon, transferring money between bank accounts electronically, or even paying your bills online. However, here we are using a narrower definition that pertains to Shadow Banking: any financial intermediaries that use electronic means of gathering and disseminating funds outside of the formal banking system.

In China, the bulk of online Shadow Banking consists of peer-to-peer (P2P) lending. P2P lenders are online organizations that act as online conduits, or financial intermediaries, between borrowers and lenders. Globally, the industry got its start in 2005 with the first P2P platform, Zopa, in the UK Later, the Lending Club and Prosper rose to dominance in the US market. In China, the first platforms were launched in 2007, with a small group of several dozen companies and total lending of $100 million. There have been booms and busts in the industry since then as small firms took advantage of the country's wealth, rapidly increasing mobile telephone networks, and a regulatory black hole. However, starting with China's $600 billion stimulus in 2009, the flood of cash into the country's financial institutions caused a huge surge in P2P platforms. By 2015, there were approximately 600 platforms with more joining every day, charging anywhere from 15 percent to 40 percent in interest to their borrowers.

The advantage of P2P companies is twofold. First, they are incredibly convenient. Borrowers and lenders alike can shift fractions of money with a few simple taps on a mobile phone, an attractive feature for a culture (China) whose prime means of communication are mobile telephones. Second, they strip out the cumbersome process of personal knowledge of the creditor and rely on consumer behavior data that—at least theoretically—allows them to manage risk at low cost.

Apart from the fast-rising internet companies, more established financial institutions, like banks, gradually entered the online market. These included China Merchants Bank, Ping An Bank, and Citic Bank. Their business models differed in terms of due diligence and customer base, but they share a similar concept of online financial intermediation. As with WMPs sold by the banks, these products distributed by formal financial institutions could be considered Shadow Loans because the banks were merely acting as an intermediary between lender and borrower and the actual capital did not sit on the bank's balance sheet.

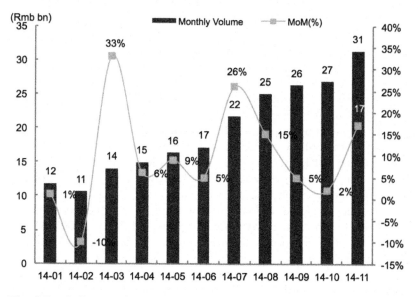

Fig. 9.1   Online Lenders in China (*Source*: Company Data)

***

In 2012, I took a trip to the lovely city of Hangzhou, two hours west of Shanghai. Hangzhou is famous for its West Lake, a scenic spot to sightsee while crossing the stone bridge that links the two edges of the lake. One of my favorite hotels is the Shangri-la overseeing the lake, a plush place with a pagoda on top and Russian style architecture below, built in the 1950s just as Mao came to power. I would sit in the top-floor executive lounge imagining Henry Kissinger, who stayed there, sipping tea while discussing global politics with Mao. Apart from the beauty of the city, Hangzhou is also known as the home of Alibaba, the Amazon of China—and also owner of China's largest P2P company. Alibaba's founder, Jack Ma, is an iconoclastic entrepreneur known for his integrity. He's also been able to thrive while building his multi-billion dollar company through much rumored connections with the top leaders in Beijing and a willingness to play by the unofficial rules of adherence to the Communist Party when necessary. After dropping out of school three times, he traveled to the USA in the mid-1990s where he discovered the internet. But it was an internet that had few searchable terms in China. So with $20,000 in seed money from his wife and a friend, he launched Alibaba. He's become China's richest man with a $24 billion fortune.

I traveled to Hangzhou with a New York City hedge fund manager to visit Alibaba. The headquarters in Hangzhou was built by an international architecture firm, called Hassell, and looks like a collection of giant spider webs; the campus was in tune with the vibe of Silicon Valley. The place felt a lot more like Google than a typical low-cost internet company in China, which are usually hidden in a warren of rooms in a nondescript office building.

We were there not to visit the executives at the company that sold goods online, which is Alibaba's main business. Instead, we wanted to see Alibaba's finance arm. We had arranged to speak with the head of a tiny operation that I thought of as Alibaba's bank—one of the earliest online Shadow Banks. We had inklings that this new financial services business could be a game changer in China. Later, Alibaba would form a company called Ant Financial, that included a host of online businesses, including the popular Alipay online payment system. Ant eventually grew to be worth more than $60 billion, with 600 million users offering a host of services including third-party payment, fund sales, banking, insurance, personal credit, and securities. In 2016, Ant Financial managed to raise $4.5 billion from Chinese investors, including the country's sovereign wealth fund, China Investment Corp., and China Construction Bank. However, at the time we visited, this plan was barely a gleam in Jack Ma's eye.

Alibaba's online bank was born of a simple but brilliant idea. Alibaba's transaction business contained a database of millions of people who have launched small online businesses selling goods. Every time an item is bought or sold, the price, value, and total quantity are totted up in Alibaba's computers. Why not tap into this database to mine for companies in good financial health that were seeking capital for expansion? And use the vast treasure trove of data to analyze credit risk? Figure out who are the good potential borrowers and which ones might be bad apples?

Alibaba's bank started with 1.2 billion renminbi of capital in 2011, rising to 2.2 billion renminbi in January 2012. By 2014, the business had arranged more than $100 billion (600 billion renminbi) in online funding.

As the business grew, because of its tremendous scale and the company's huge visibility within China, Alibaba became the guinea pig of China's online finance industry. However, this growth did not come without costs. Even during our visits my suspicions were raised about how diligent the firm was about "knowing the customer." Alibaba claimed it could analyze risk carefully. But when we asked about the risk profile of the firm's borrowers—given the slowing economy and spate of rate cuts at the time of our visit—an Alibaba executive said the firm had not changed its lending rates, which was surprising given the variability of risks of the borrower. What interest were they charging during our visit? 18 percent. What did they charge the previous year? 18 percent. It didn't sound like they were analyzing risk so much as they were shoveling cash out the door.

Several years later, as I focused my analysis increasingly on China's blossoming Shadow Banking industry, my team and I took another close look at Alibaba's online bank. What we found confirmed my earlier fears. What was designed to be a careful use of data to sift through the borrowers to filter out the good from the bad, looked increasingly like a giant funnel pouring money into the riskiest borrowers in the shakiest sectors. And the reason was simple: high yields. The only way to attract lenders in the boom years of China's economy was to prove that you could provide the highest returns. And the highest returns tended to come from the most aggressive borrowers. This is the essence of Shadow Banking in China—online or in the offline banks. Shadow Banks must compete with established lenders and so they tend to operate in the economic sectors that offer the highest return and concomitantly the highest potential for defaults.

Alibaba's financial arm, which was eventually renamed Yuebao (pronounced U A Bow) provided a breakdown in 2014 of their loan book.

This ostensibly consisted of very safe investments: 92 percent bank deposits, 4 percent bonds, 3 percent financial assets such as repurchase agreements and other items. This would be reassuring to investors. They could move their money by tapping a few keys into their phone for very high returns in what appeared to be rock solid investments. But we were skeptical. So we started digging.

What we discovered was worrisome. The high yields Yuebao was offering to customers were unattainable unless it was investing in much risker financial products than bank deposits and bonds. While it was difficult to prove, because Yuebao did not provide much detail, it looked much like what we had witnessed among the Trusts and other Shadow Lenders—a firm chasing shaky financial investments.

One Shanghai investment banker familiar with the online investments issued by Yuebao said their quite high seven-day annualized interest rate was unlikely given their stated investment in safe bank products called negotiated deposits. These are deposits whose interest rate is "negotiated" between the banks and the investors. "We have monitored Yuebao's seven-day annualized interest rate for a while and found the average was much higher than the interest rate of negotiated savings deposits for the same period. If these funds were invested in our accounts, it would be impossible for Yuebao to maintain an interest rate above this level, which we have never offered them," he told us (Author Interview 2015).

If Yuebao was not putting the money to work in ordinary stocks and bonds, where was it going? As they did not disclose this information, we had to make some educated guesses. The most probable destination for the funds collected would have been the extremely hot property market, many of whose projects were connected to the famously risky LGFVs. Only this sector—at least at the time of our research—would have generated such high returns. Clearly, the potential for default was much higher with these speculative property projects than for ordinary stocks or bonds.

That was the first red flag: confusion about the investment destination. A second issue that arose was non-transparent cross-ownership. This is where there is a relationship between the financial intermediary collecting the funds and the company that is using the capital. This is a clear conflict of interest and in most well-regulated markets must be spelled out. If my firm says it is an independent financial company, it is supposed to be independent of any fund. If it is actually raising money for a project owned by a sister company then that is going to make investors suspicious that I am not acting as an independent broker. This issue has cropped up in the USA. Financial advisors sometimes sell products that their investment banks have created. Who knows if these products are a good buy if they are being promoted by the bank? Due to this potential for conflict of interest, the Chinese Shadow Banks, including Yuebao, usually do not spell this out. We spotted this problem with Yuebao.

What was Yuebao promising? Here's where it gets a bit complicated. The website referred to another fund. "Deposits made in Yuebao will be used to purchase a monetary fund product named Zenglibao." Zenglibao was created by a financial company called Tian Hong Asset Management. According to Tian Hong's website, "Tian Hong mainly invests in low-risk financial products such as Treasury Bonds and negotiated bank deposits." Tian Hong's website said its Zenglibao product was invested in fixed income (4.01 percent), financial asset buybacks or repos (3.5 percent), negotiated bank deposits (92.32 percent), and others (0.18 percent). There is no mention of Shadow Banking investments such as Wealth Management Products or Trusts. This all looked safe and above board—but was it?

During an interview with China's Caixin Magazine, a Tian Hong fund manager threw more confusion on to the page.

> We allocate investments and match maturities based on data analysis. At different stages a bank's ability to take deposits varies. On the one hand, there are banks that can only take, say, 10 billion yuan, but we have 11 billion yuan that needs to be taken care of. That is when we hit the limit of their deposit-taking ability. We can deal with other banks or lower the interest rates we charge. On the other hand, a larger size brings greater negotiating power. We can ask for higher interest rates. (Bing 2014)

The Tian Hong fund manager was essentially arguing that the large size of its fund gave it a strong bargaining position with the banks eager for the capital. So Tian Hong could demand a higher interest rate. But the gap was so large between the average bank deposit interest rate (around 3 percent at the time) and what Yuebao was offering its customers (around 18 percent) that it stretches the imagination to think the banks would be willing to pay enough that much in interest.

We dug a little deeper. We found information about a similar Yuebao online wealth management product launched in April 2014. The product was only available to registered Yuebao customers and was given the fancy title "Yuebao users' exclusive rights and interests II." (For some reason, Chinese Shadow Banking products have long and bizarre names—like stamping a fancy label on an ordinary bottle of water to make it look like a luxury good.)

This product was distributed in a venture with Chinese life insurance company, PRL. Investors were allowed to purchase up to 2000 units, each with a par value of 1000 renminbi. The yield was advertised as above 7 percent. However, we spoke to an executive at PRL who told a different story. He said that only the principal and a maximum of 2.5 percent annualized rate of return were guaranteed. In order to drive up the yield, Yuebao was investing only a portion of the funds in safe, low-interest products, with the rest going into the risky Shadow Banking market. And whatever the investment was would have had to generate high returns to make up for the paltry 2.5 percent offered by the guaranteed portion.

As we kept sniffing around, we discovered a winding money trail. There were a lot of what analysts call "Related Party Transactions" between the finance group and their investments that weren't explained to investors. Related Party Transactions are agreements between individuals or companies that have a personal or financial relationship. Under US Securities regulation, this has to be clearly spelled out because these can affect the investment.

According to our interviews with officials at PRL, capital raised from Yuebao II was to be allocated to infrastructure and property projects owned by the PRL's major shareholders: Guangdong Zhujiang Investment Company, Yuecai Trust Company, New South, Hanjian Construction Investment Company, and Guangzhou Finance Holdings Group. Two of these shareholders, Yuecai Trust and Guangzhou Financing Holdings, were owned by local governments. The rest of the shareholders belonged to the "Zhujiang Group" owned by a property magnate named Zhu Mengyi and his family. Zhu Mengyi also controlled the Hong Kong-listed Hopson Development (754 HK). According to media reports, the group had a habit of rolling over debt to resolve liquidity problems, a real no-no in financial circles, because it meant he couldn't afford to pay the interest.

The main businesses of the Zhuhai group were property and infrastructure. However, to offset the group's declining revenue in these areas and to replenish working capital, finance and insurance became the major contributors to revenue.

So, far from investments in safe products like bank savings, it appeared the Zhujiang group was using Yuebao to collect funds to invest in financial speculation and to fund its daily operations—what analysts call working capital. Based on insurance rules, this was legal—but highly risky.

Although rules issued by the PBOC, the CSRC, and the CBRC had by then eliminated most opportunities for publicly raised funds to invest in non-standard financial projects, universal life insurance was one of the few sectors left that still allowed this. Because the rules on insurance premium investments were more relaxed, universal life insurance products tended to be a far higher liability than other types of Shadow Banking investments. Most existing universal insurance products at the time were investing in low-risk financial instruments such as bonds. By investing in property and LGFVs, PRL was functioning more like a Trust company. However, unlike Trusts, PRL didn't have to disclose detailed investment information to investors. The product didn't pass the smell test for safety.

Alibaba duplicated this unorthodox model for its own online investment products. In April 2014, Alibaba launched a new product called Yulebao (Pronounced "U L Bow" and not to be confused with the company Yuebao). The fund marketed its new financial product as an investment in the entertainment industry ("Yulebao lets you pay 200 Yuan for being a movie fan!"). But the funds were *also* put into insurance products. According to our interviews with insurance executives, funds raised through Yulebao were placed in the wealth and insurance funds of another insurance firm, Guohua Life Insurance. This made the investment appear "safe." However, then Guohua turned around and put the money into Trust products; Guohua didn't say which ones. At the time, Yuebao and its parent Alibaba would not reveal to the public the Trust company's name, the terms of the underlying trust products, or the underlying projects. They said these were "trade secrets."

Bottom line, investors were content to trust the investment companies' brand names—like Alibaba—and assumed the asset risk was low. But they were wrong. And it was hard to tell how risky because there was very little disclosure.

***

Fast Money—and Fraud—Online

Noah Holdings Takes Risks

Although the online landscape has been littered with fly-by-night companies that collapsed under the weight of their illicit ambitions, some managed to rise to greater heights. One success story has been Noah Holdings.

The once fledgling company, started in 2007, became big enough to go public on the New York Stock Exchange and achieve a market capitalization of more than one billion dollars. But did it really succeed through smart management—or did it start to play some of the same games that we've seen with others in the industry? Burrowing into Noah's financial statements, we unearthed a host of issues that pointed to some of the broader problems with China's Shadow Banking. As competition for deposits rose, and more and more companies jumped into the fray, the smaller firms like Noah strove to compete by taking greater risks in their investments. And because the regulators were always rushing to catch up to the industry, there were plenty of opportunities to sidestep the rules. There was no one minding the store.

At the time of our analysis in 2015, Noah had three lines of business. First, there were one-time commissions from Wealth Management Products (WMP), bought by wealthy individuals or corporations. Second, Noah earned fees paid by third parties to access Noah's online client base. And third, Noah received service fees, paid by mutual funds and other outside firms to distribute their financial products.

As we sniffed through Noah's financial statements, we soon noticed a curious fall in active users. Just as Twitter began peaking after scooping up all of the available twitter customers, Noah soon discovered that the number of active users—people who bought and sold financial products through Noah's online system—began slowing down. In our research, we calculated that, by the end of 2015, although the registered clients were growing at a healthy 30 percent clip, the *active* users were beginning to decline. After years of pell-mell growth, by the third quarter of 2015, active clients totaled 4014, down a sharp 34 percent from the second quarter. We were even told by a manager at a competitor of Noah that a large portion of the newly registered accounts were actually created by the company itself to embellish the operating metrics, although this was difficult to prove.

But the biggest issue with Noah was not its growth but the way it conducted its business. Most Shadow Banks—including online ones like Noah—are quick to say that their investments are "safe" and sometimes even "guaranteed." But for the ordinary investor, they're turning to these operators mainly because they offered high returns. Why put your money in a bank for a paltry 3 percent when you can get double digits from the Shadow Banks?

Initially, Noah put a big chunk of the money it was given into safe investments like bonds. But bonds tend to offer low interest rates. In order to maintain the growth of its wealth management business, Noah started to move money into less safe investments. One of the biggest was called private equity. Private equity is simply buying into a business that has not yet sold shares to the public—hence the name *private*. Obviously, since it is has no tradable shares, you can't wake up one day and sell your company stock. You're stuck with the investment until you can locate another buyer. The other devilish detail was that the biggest target investment for private equity in China at the time was the property market—which was rapidly moving into a downward spiral. The change in product mix was the classic trade-off between risk and growth. Private equity WMPs distributed by Noah were mainly composed of (1) private equity funds sponsored by domestic and international fund management firms, (2) real estate funds and fund of funds managed by the company itself, and (3) asset management plans sponsored by mutual fund management companies or securities companies, the underlying assets of which are portfolios of equity investments in unlisted private enterprises.

That didn't stop Noah. Determined to keep the cash coming in, Noah almost quadrupled the proportion of private equity-related financial products from only 10 percent in the third quarter of 2014 to 39 percent in the third quarter of 2015. As a result, the proportion of bond investments dropped significantly from the peak of 74 percent in the beginning of 2014 to 29 percent by the end of 2015.

Moreover, we also discovered that Noah was telling its customers it was a middleman—when in fact it was raising money for its own funds. This is very similar to a Merrill Lynch financial advisor advising its customers on how to manage retirement money—but then putting it into Merrill Lynch funds. That's a no-no in the West.

The largest proportion of Noah's high-risk real estate funds was managed by the company's own asset management platform, called Gopher. In 2014, Gopher only accounted for 39 percent of transactions, while independent funds were 61 percent. A year and a half later, that was reversed—Gopher suddenly took 68 percent of funds. And not surprisingly, Gopher started putting the money into the higher risk "other" category of investments. "Noah is famous for its real estate funds. In fact, the latest property boom gave the company its current success and a leading position in the industry," said the CEO of a wealth management company in Shanghai (Author Interview 2015). Noah first started real estate funds in 2012 with assets of 7.2 billion renminbi and within a year had tripled that to 23.9 billion renminbi.

There was a proliferation of related party transactions, another forbidden ploy. In 2014, an asset management plan called "Wanjia Win-Win," distributed by Noah, employed an outside fund manager, Jingtai Management. The fund, which dubbed itself "the safest asset management plan," was established by Wanjia Win-Win Assets Management, a joint venture in which Noah's own company, Gopher, held a 35 percent stake, along with another fund, Shenzhen Jingtai Fund Management. Noble Equity Investment Fund (Shanghai) Management, also a subsidiary of Noah, acted as the plan's investment advisor. Noah distributed the plan among its wealthy investors. As the result of its ownership stakes, Noah enjoyed a much higher commission rate. However, there was no independent, hands-off relationship between the middleman raising the funds (Noah) and the investment funds. "In addition, the risk controls have been very loose," a senior manager at You Choose Wealth, an independent advisory firm, told our researchers.

As the risky investments rose, even financial analysts within China became increasingly concerned. "We expect a symbolic risk event to happen soon, which would attract the regulator's attention and thus lead to the introduction of new rules for the industry," an independent financial analyst said during an interview (Author Interview 2015).

Noah was an example of an industry-wide trend. Since the explosion of credit following the 2009 stimulus, many new companies had become distributors of financial products, outside of the official banking system. These companies, including online and offline firms, were chasing deposits by offering high yields. These high yields have been achieved through increasingly risky and non-transparent methods, and thus add to the systemic risks already embedded in China's Shadow Banking market.

* * *

So with the Wild West of Shadow Banking came equally wild and wooly defaults. The most bizarre case of P2P gone wild was a company called Yucheng International Holdings. In January 2016, the press reported that Yucheng was under investigation for "illegally taking deposits from the public," all told more than 40 billion renminbi from 800,000 people. Nine employees were arrested. That charge was punishable by death until late in 2015, when a legal amendment changed the maximum sentence to life in prison. Yucheng was a striking example of how the regulators had little oversight over where these online firms put investors' money.

Yucheng reportedly sent nearly 10 billion renminbi to Myanmar's Wa State, a conflict-torn area bordering the southwestern province of Yunnan known to be one of the largest sources of heroin. It was never clear how the company spent that money (South China Morning Post 2016a).

Yucheng's founder, a man named Ding, was born in the eastern province of Anhui and later became a citizen of Myanmar (Burma). He led an "extremely luxurious" life and had relationships with several women who worked for him. Ding gave Zhang Min, the president of Yucheng's subsidiary, called Ezubo, several hundred million renminbi worth of real estate and cash, according to a report in Reuters. Xie Jie, who headed a corporate committee in charge of preparing for the establishment of a Free Trade Zone in Myanmar, was given properties worth tens of millions of renminbi from Ding (Reuters 2016).

Adding fuel to the fire, Ding built up a power base in his home province of Anhui. Investigators began probing the links between Yucheng and government officials in Bengbu, the city in Anhui where the firm was headquartered until moving to Beijing in 2015. In an odd demonstration of its power, Yucheng founded what it called a "militia group" in Bengbu. Officials from the People's Liberation Army in the city and the local government reportedly attended a ceremony founding the group. Wherever Ding went, his bodyguards followed, with a haul of cash to "lubricate relationships," Reuters noted. This is a classic example of a hometown entrepreneur making it big and then corrupting local officials.

For all of 2015, 950 P2P companies defaulted. In the early part of 2016, more companies went under, including E leasing, DADA group, Anhao Group, Rongye Network, Agriculture Capital, Financing center, Huika Century, and Xinliyuan, for a total of 70 billion renminbi. That's a significant level of defaults, losing almost 10 billion renminbi.

***

Beijing Comes to the Rescue

China's regulators aren't blind when the finance industry runs into brick walls. They are quite a sophisticated group, particularly at the PBOC. The CSRC, however, has tended to lightly regulate the securities industry. When I was first an investment banker in Hong Kong in the late 1990s, I knew many Hong Kong financiers who were plucked from the hurly burly world of investment banking to move to Shanghai to work with the CSRC. Since many of the senior people were accustomed to Hong Kong's strict securities laws, the CSRC was relatively disciplined in overseeing Chinese securities firms. However, over time, many of the Hong Kong-trained regulators left Shanghai, and their positions were taken over by less well-trained PRC nationals. Given the ups and downs of the market, there have been many rumors of cases of insider trading that the CSRC has been unable to halt.

Apart from internal issues among regulators, there is also a reluctance among the leadership itself to confront new industries. As with any country, there is infighting among different groups about how rules should be set, particularly in an industry as new and fast growing as online finance. Thus, it is no surprise that the regulators were slow to tackle online finance. The regulators even encouraged a light touch on this fast-moving industry. According to the respected Caixin Magazine in Beijing, an internet financing sector policy paper issued in 2015 by the PBOC, the Ministry of Finance, the Ministry of Industry and Information Technology and other ministries said P2P websites should be regulated as private lenders and allowed to do business with fewer restrictions than banks and other traditional financial institutions (Caixin 2015).

During the June 2015 conference I attended in Beijing, entitled "Inclusive Financial Innovation," I was struck by the passionate commitment among officials and academics for online finance. They genuinely viewed it as a vehicle to provide access to capital for rural entrepreneurs, who, for most of China's post-reform history, have been starved of money. Unfortunately, much of the industry has been hijacked by entrepreneurs among the fast money crowd in the cities who have been able to woo investors to plunk down savings for risky property projects.

In 2014 and into 2015, regulators began strengthening their oversight of the industry, aiming for a full set of standards by mid-2016.

Among the proposals, the PBOC would stipulate that single money transfers through individual third-party payment accounts could not exceed 1,000 renminbi, and cumulative yearly transfers could not exceed 10,000 renminbi. Single purchases wouldn't exceed 5,000 renminbi, and total monthly purchases would be below 10,000 renminbi. While additional details were sketchy at the time of writing, the CBRC would require P2P website operators to adopt risk control standards to prevent risky, loan-concentration practices through which some firms have bundled investor loans for large-scale borrowers. The CBRC also wished to push local governments to take the lead in supervising P2P businesses in their respective regions. The commission's regulators, meanwhile, would provide risk monitoring and warn the industry when problems arise (Caixin, ibid., December 10, 2016).

The new rules would improve risk controls and better information disclosure. Caixin speculated that the CBRC would be likely to lay the groundwork for a "negative list" approach to supervising businesses while leaving ample room for innovation. The negative list is important in China; it permits all behavior not specifically prohibited, which limits the government's ability to jump in without warning. There was talk of including clauses aimed at preventing website operators from raising funds, offering asset securitization products, and coordinating loans for clients whose identifies cannot be verified.

Apart from obligations to protect investors, the regulators also have been extremely concerned about cases of fraud; massive online defaults could lead to social unrest. This is particularly true of online investing where individual cases can go viral and spark nationwide protests. There have been several instances of online fraud that set off widespread protests that are likely to have concerned the leadership.

The Guangdong-based University of Jinan issued a report at the beginning of 2016 that cited internet financial fraud as a greater concern than land compensation, labor disputes, pollution, rows over property ownership, and medical conflicts. One major case cited by Jinan was a series of protests among investors sparked by alleged fraud at the Fanya Metals Exchange based in Yunnan province. The case involved 40 billion renminbi assembled from 220,000 investors from 20 provinces, the report noted, citing a Chinese newspaper called the Securities Daily. A protest staged on September 2015 saw more than 1000 people gather outside the State Bureau for Letters and Calls, the department responsible for handling petitions to the government. The protests lasted for months. One investor from Shanxi province who was outside the bureau for letters and calls told the South China Morning Post: "I'm here to sign for my family. They lost more than 200,000 renminbi. An uncle of mine lost 10 million renminbi, another 8 renminbi." Another investor from Sichuan province said she invested after seeing documents that appeared to officially endorse the metal exchange. "More than a dozen of us came [from Sichuan]. We lost about 2 million renminbi in total, but the government said nothing. We almost invested all our life savings after we saw official documents that endorsed the company" (South China Morning Post 2016b).

These incidents led the central government to step in with additional measures to oversee the industry. The Communist Party agency that oversees the courts and police launched a nationwide crackdown to clean up internet finance schemes. The Central Political and Legal Affairs Commission told its local offices to set up teams to handle cases of alleged internet financial fraud. Shanghai along with Shandong and Jiangsu provinces has already set up "leading groups" to improve the supervision of internet fund-raising schemes.

THE BANKS FIGHT BACK

The banks in China eyed the rapid rise of internet finance with dread. As we discussed earlier, they jumped into the Shadow Banking game with their own Wealth Management Products once they saw the handwriting on the wall; they would lose depositors unless they offered similar financial products. The same thinking has occurred among the banks about internet finance. They certainly were not going to take a challenge from the Shadow Banking sector—particularly one with a sexy name like "internet" attached to it—lying down. The banks have had two important weapons on their side: size and power. The tremendous reach of the banks across China gives them a scale that even the internet companies cannot match, although clearly over time the whole point of internet finance is to bypass physical limitations and reach the market electronically. With 220,000 branches, the banks, both state and private, have a power base in cities and townships across the country. The second advantage is that the banks are so important to the financial system that they have a lot of pull with the PBOC and even the top leaders in the State Council. The leaders know that capital flows are the lifeblood of the state and the banks are central to that.

✶ ✶ ✶

As with WMPs, internet finance had the potential to cause deposits to decline at the commercial banks. Faced with intense competition for retail deposits from Yuebao and other online lenders, banks in China took measures to ward off the threat. They established test branches for their own money market products and they also set daily limits for depositors to transfer funds to online companies. Banks including Ping An Bank, Communications Bank of China, Industrial and Commercial Bank of China, Bank of China, China Minsheng Banking Corp began selling their own money market products online. More banks soon followed suit.

Many listed banks began noting in their financial statements that their operating profits were affected by internet financing due to the loss of deposits. For example, in its financial statements for the first half of 2015, the Bank of China said:

> In response to external changes such as further interest rate liberalization **and the rapid development of internet finance,** the Bank vigorously ... pushed forward the stable growth of deposits based on the strength of the Group's diversified financial services. (Bank of China Financial Statements 2015)

Bank deposits had been declining. But there is a debate about whether the banks actually did lose market share to online finance. Let's look at the data for one period. Total deposits at 12 listed banks increased 9.8 per cent from 58.75 trillion renminbi in 2012 to 64.49 trillion renminbi in 2013. The comparable number for 2011 was 51.14 trillion renminbi, for a 14.9 percent growth from 2010. Clearly, there was a slowdown in deposit growth for the banks.

In addition, for the first time since China started enjoying rapidly rising GDP growth, 8 of 12 listed banks reported a lower percentage of demand deposits, which are funds that can be withdrawn at any time, such as by writing a check. By the end of 2013, there were 104.4 trillion renminbi deposited within Chinese financial institutions, of which individual demand deposits accounted for 17 percent, while corporate demand deposits stood at around 14 percent. The rest sat in term deposit accounts. Based on these numbers, if 20 percent of the individual deposits went to money market funds, which would include online finance, this would represent 3.55 trillion renminbi and 2.92 trillion renminbi. We admit these numbers are speculative.

Chinese banks have had an easy ride. For decades, they were the only place where the average citizen could put his or her money and get a return. But the returns were meager because the banks did not have to offer more. As we discussed earlier, financial repression meant the lending and borrowing rates were fixed by the PBOC—the average Chinese saver didn't have a choice. Shadow Banking, along with online finance, changed that. All of a sudden, the banks faced competition. They didn't like that because the new policies hurt their profits.

For example, in 2012, banks originally only had to pay 0.35 percent interest on demand deposits. However, online finance forced them to increase the interest they offered, because depositors could take their demand deposits from their banking accounts and give them to online companies like Alibaba's Yuebao, or other financial intermediaries.

In the case of Alibaba's Yuebao, the banks were eager to tap into the internet companies' vast database of investors. However, the only way they could do that was by increasing the interest rates offered. The online finance firms started raising money from investors and putting it into the banks, negotiating with the banks about the interest payments. The banks agreed to do this—but at a huge cost. Instead of paying out 1 or 2 percent in interest, they suddenly had to pay a whopping 6 percent interest for these so-called negotiated deposit accounts. Although the capital flowed back to banks, they were paying nearly triple what they usually paid on savings deposits—in 2014 this amounted to another 5.65 percent. This impacted the banks' key profit center—the interest rate differential between deposits and loans.

How much money was this? According to the financial filings of Yuebao's asset management arm, called Tianhong, in the fourth quarter of 2013, fully 92.21 percent of Tianhong's funds were invested in these negotiated bank deposits. Thus, for just one internet company alone (albeit a very large one), Yuebao put a whopping 170 billion renminbi into the banks (although, as we mentioned, we are not sure how accurate these figures were). If we assume the interest rate was around 5.5 percent, the banks were paying a significantly higher amount of interest—around 9.35 billion renminbi. This truly was capitalism at its finest. Suddenly, the banks were chasing the internet companies and paying a hefty premium to boot.

Because Shadow Banking has been a very hot market in China, the competition became fierce between the online financial intermediaries and other Shadow Banks that were lending money. Alibaba may have been paying out even more interest than it was receiving from the banks. Yuebao could have been losing money in order for the parent, Alibaba, to gain market share in financial services. We think the company was expecting to introduce other, more profitable products once it gained sufficient market share.

THE FUTURE OF ONLINE FINANCE IN CHINA

What is the future of online finance in China? Will it contribute to the growth of capitalism or will it be sideswiped by the big state banks and/ or sink into the ocean of fraud that seems to have enveloped the industry since its start? For a start, we can look at comparisons with the experience of other emerging countries.

Kellee Tsai, a professor at the Hong Kong University of Science and Technology, has examined models of what she calls "inclusive finance" in emerging countries. Inclusive finance refers to sources of capital that are made available to others in the food chain apart from the elites in the urban cities; these groups are excluded from formal finance. Online and P2P could be one way of bringing them into the fold. This would be particularly important for the small business owners in China's rural areas who for decades have scrambled to pull together enough capital to start operating, as the banks have tended to favor the state firms. Tsai notes that China is making strides providing access to capital to a wider group, rising from 63.8 percent of the population in 2011 to 78.9 percent in 2014. This is about on par with Malaysia but far exceeds a country like Vietnam, where only 30.9 percent of the population can borrow or save money or use other services from formal banks. One of the point she makes in her research is that the formal financial institutions in places like India and Indonesia have started to use "branchless banking" through mobile devices. These services will compete with Shadow Banking in rural areas from private lenders (Tsai 2015c). But these are early days for this kind of financial intermediation in China.

* * *

Will the state win and take over internet finance? Or will the big competitors like Alibaba or small P2P shops continue to gain market share?

First, it is axiomatic that the banking system, particularly the four state-owned banks, must remain healthy. As we have indicated throughout this book, they are the lifeblood of the country—particularly to the leadership. P2P and online finance in general will be allowed to grow but cannot threaten the viability of the core of the financial system—the banks. That means at some point the State Council, acting through the CBRC and the PBOC, will curtail the growth of online finance by independent companies.

Online transactions company Alibaba ($153 billion market cap) and search company Baidu ($53 billion market cap) were allowed to flourish because they did not threaten any existing, politically powerful state firms. Online transaction companies like Alibaba threaten retailers, but apart from the Cosco Group, there are no major state players in this arena.

The same is true of search giant Baidu; search did affect advertising for the one giant in media, China Central Television (CCTV), but the CCTV has been able to maintain its revenue because it has a monopoly on the top television channels in China. State firms, and even private firms, feel duty bound to advertise on CCTV to promote themselves to local and Beijing leaders, as much as to the population at large. The other media enterprises, such as provincial television networks and newspapers, have been too scattered to provide much opposition to Baidu. Baidu itself was a multi-headed hydra that crossed so many segments of commerce that it was difficult for any opposition to chop off any one head.

That is not true for online finance. Financial flows are very much the domain of the state, and the banks operate as the state's banker. They cannot be infringed upon.

For our purposes, when we speak of online finance we are focusing narrowly on Shadow Banking and the rise of capitalism, not all forms of online financial intermediation. The state may not wish to allow non-state entities to take dominant market share away from the banks, but they do see a role for online finance to provide capital to certain sectors. These include the rural population and SMEs. Throughout its post-revolution history China has heavily concentrated its economy on the growth of heavy industry, concentrated primarily in large cities and in the north. Other areas of the country, including the west, parts of the middle of the country, and even some portions of the south, have been neglected in the country's race to modernize through industrialization. The 1980s liberalization under Deng Xiaoping succeeded in part by allowing small businesses to flourish in many regions outside of the core urban centers, where the population often was heavily wedded to the state structure— the so-called Iron Rice Bowl. Later decades, however, saw a decline in this growth. With a slowing economy, China may need to turn to new forms of financial intermediation in order to deliver capital to these capital-starved regions and sectors. Online financial intermediation could be one helpful tool.

CHAPTER 10

The Risks of Shadow Banking

In 2012, the government-owned *China Daily* newspaper published an opinion piece that was startling in its frankness. It was written by the chairman of the Bank of China, Xiao Gang, an official not known for brash talk. In it, he praised "Shadow Banking activities that have allowed many projects to obtain fresh funds and hence avoid default," and said "this could be one of the major reasons why the formal banking system in general is still enjoying declining non-performing loan ratios, despite the weakening repayment capabilities of some borrowers."

But he also warned that "in order to prevent China's financial systemic or regional risks from happening, it is imperative to pay more attention to shadow banking and to enhance supervision over shadow banking activities" (Gang, http://www.chinadaily.com.cn/opinion/2012-10/12/content_15812305.htm).

Anne Stevenson-Yang, one of the most astute analysts of China's economy, has warned that a crisis is on the way—and Shadow Banking could be one catalyst:

> The steps the leaders have taken and are now ramping up even more will actually make the coming financial crisis worse. That is because bailouts have maintained bloated asset values, and leveraged up step by step, from one bloated asset class to another, pulling taut the ties that bind assets, such that now, when one goes it will cause a chain reaction. (Stevenson-Yang 2015)

© The Author(s) 2017
A. Collier, *Shadow Banking and the Rise of Capitalism in China*,
DOI 10.1007/978-981-10-2996-7_10

But the key issue that will define Shadow Banking is China's slowing economy and high levels of debt. These are starting to constrain activity among all institutions.

Will Shadow Banking cause a collapse of the Chinese economy?

Throughout this book we have argued that Shadow Banking allowed Beijing to simultaneously paper over the cracks in China's fiscal system and provide capital for the country's private entrepreneurs. But Shadow Banking could also be a catalyst for the failure of the Chinese economy. This is what economists call systemic risk—the collapse of an entire financial system rather than of one sector or financial intermediary. Commentators such as Gordon Chang, the author of "The Coming Collapse of China," for years has warned that China was likely to hit a financial meltdown due to excessive debt and other problems. What are the risks caused by Shadow Banking in China?

Chinese Shadow Banking is a very different creature from that in other countries. For example, the American mortgage crisis was a creature of Shadow Banking. However, American Shadow Banking was essentially a flow of funds *between* non-banks (Shadow Banks). These non-banks included a number of institutions, including investment banks that diced mortgages into small pieces, each with its own risk profile, and then sold them to investment and retirement funds, along with local mortgage brokers, who persuaded ordinary customers to take out mortgages beyond their income levels, which were then bundled into others for packaging by the investment banks. The money that caused the crisis was essentially sloshing around between these financial intermediaries. Economist Zoltan Pozsar of the George Soros-funded Institute for New Economic Thinking notes that at the height of the financial crisis in 2007 the American economy held $22 trillion of Shadow Banking liabilities. He describes the process thusly:

> The shadow banking system is organized around securitization and whole-sale funding. In the shadow banking system, loans, leases, and mortgages are securitized and thus become tradable instruments. Funding is also in the form of tradable instruments, such as commercial paper and repo. Savers hold money market balances, instead of deposits with banks. Like the traditional banking system, the shadow banking system conducts credit intermediation. However, unlike the traditional banking system, where credit intermediation is performed "under one roof"—that of a bank—in

the shadow banking system, it is performed *through a daisy-chain of non-bank financial intermediaries* in a multi step process. These steps entail the "vertical slicing" of traditional banks' credit intermediation process. (Pozsar 2010)

Economists have called this the *financialization* of the American economy. According to Nobel Prize-winning economist Robert Solow, "Any complicated economy needs a complicated financial system: to allocate dispersed capital to dispersed productive uses, to provide liquidity, to do maturity and risk transformation, and to produce market evaluations of uncertain prospects. If these functions are not performed adequately, the economy cannot produce and grow with anything like efficiency. Granted all that, however, the suspicion persists that financialization has gone too far" (Solow 2013).

Historian Perry Mehrling puts it slightly differently, saying that "The crisis was a stress test of shadow banking, money market funding of capital market lending" (Mehrling 2016).

In China, Shadow Banking is not a creature of finance or "capital market lending," as Merhling declares. The "daisy chain" of funds between financial intermediaries does exist in China, but it is relatively small compared to the West. Instead, Shadow Banking in China is a stepchild of the mainstream banking system. Most of the capital loaned by Shadow Banks is invested directly into the real economy. Because China's financial markets are much less well developed than in the West, there are fewer opportunities for banks to dream up fancy new financial products. Chinese Shadow Banks are mostly just banks without regulation. Shadow Banking in China is mostly a three-tiered system of institutions that act like banks: formal institutions like banks, smaller financial firms like guarantee companies and pawn shops, and finally, informal finance like personal loans between individuals (Li and Hsu 2014).

China's low level of development of its financial markets has made the banks the centerpiece of Shadow Banking. "In China, shadow banking relies on traditional banks to perform many basic functions of credit intermediation. This makes it very 'bank-centric', and a true 'shadow' of the banking system. In contrast, capital markets have long been an integral part of the US financial system and have provided an efficient platform for financial innovation" (Dang et al. 2015a).

The exception to this rule are the Shadow Banking products that have been invested in the stock market, which was one of the contributing factors to the rapid rise (and fall) of the Chinese equity markets in the summer of 2015. However, investors weren't buying fancy products—just company shares. Nor were these giant pools of capital diced and sliced into fancy derivatives. Company shares are a breed apart from the complex mortgage derivatives that stalled the American economy.

We can see this in the small size of China's financial markets, in contrast to the USA. The American stock market is around 130 percent of GDP, compared to around 50 percent for China. As we have noted, the country's finances are dominated by the Big Four state-owned banks—and increasingly by the Shadow Banks. Where stock and bond markets play a crucial role in the West, in China banks run the financial system.

In 2015, China's domestic stock market supplied 760 billion renminbi in funding to non-financial firms. This was only 5 percent of total financing flows to the real economy. Credit in the Chinese economy rose significantly following the 2008 credit stimulus. Total financing as a proportion of GDP increased by 88 percentage points. In 2015, bank loans made up 69 percent of new financing. Meanwhile, stock market money as a proportion of GDP increased by only 3 percentage points and has averaged around 50 percent of GDP for the past few years (Yang 2016b).

However, in very recent times, China's financial system has been changing to become more like the Western. That means more "financialization." The institutions selling financial products have grown to be a bigger part of the economy. For example, margin financing for the stock market, where the buyer puts money down to buy shares but borrows the rest, has grown from 0.6 trillion renminbi in 2014 to 2.2 trillion renminbi by 2015. Stocks used as collateral for other investments reached 2 trillion renminbi. And loans between banks and between banks and other financial institutions have also skyrocketed (Liao et al. 2016b). But we believe the main problem remains the underlying economy—primarily Shadow Loans to ailing state and private firms, and to the overblown property sector.

Even though China's economy is not as "financialized" as it is in the West, there is still the potential for a crisis that could cause a rapid decline in wealth due to fundamental factors. During the US mortgage meltdown, Americans lost 16 percent of their wealth, five times more than the 3 percent lost during the Great Depression. In the fourth quarter of 2008 during the height of the crisis, GDP fell 8.3 percent. As Timothy Geithner, former Treasury Secretary during the financial crisis, noted:

The disappearance of wealth, disposable income, and jobs was dragging down private demand, which further depressed asset prices, putting more pressure on banks to hoard liquidity and restrict credit, which in turn sucked more financial oxygen out of the economy. Economic distress meant more delinquent mortgages, which meant more troubled mortgage securities weighing down banks, which meant less lending and more economic distress. This vicious cycle of financial and economic contraction was gaining momentum, and no one was sure how it would end. Fear of a depression was making a depression more likely. (Geithner 2014b)

***

One of the main issues is whether the problems within the banks and Shadow Banks become so big they become *systemic*. This means that their defaults threaten the entire economy. Federal Reserve Chairman Timothy Geithner and his colleagues felt the American banks had to be recapitalized because their failure could have hurt the entire American economy. Thus, the mortgage meltdown was considered a systemic crisis. The authors of one book on banking crises aptly summarize how the mortgage meltdown in the USA was a systemic risk to the banking system. "When the dominos are standing near one another, one piece falling can make all the others fall, too" (Admati and Hellwig 2013). In the case of the mortgage crisis, there were three problems that made the crisis globally connected: (1) banks around the world owned American mortgage products, (2) the banks had too little of their own money in the form of equity, and (3) much of the bank borrowing was short-term, loaned against longer duration projects. When fear rose, lenders withdrew their loans.

Is the same crisis likely to emerge in China? Would Shadow Banking be the prime cause, one factor, or irrelevant?

One commentator described the systemic nature Shadow Banking: "When an institution defaults on its Shadow Banking assets, it may also default on its liabilities to other institutions, resulting in a chain of defaults. We can therefore measure the systemic risk within the Shadow Banking system by how many defaults occur in the whole system as a result of this potential contagion" (Ibid., Li and Hsu 2014).

One of the prime problems is misallocation of capital. One of China's most trenchant analysts of China, Michael Pettis of Peking University, notes, "How much debt is there whose real cost exceeds the economic value created by the debt, which sector of the economy will pay for the excess, and what mechanism will ensure the necessary wealth transfer?" (Pettis 2013).

Economists like to look at a country's banks to estimate the potential for a meltdown. Two important measures are *insolvency* and *liquidity*. Liquidity risk is the risk that a financial firm cannot meet its cash and collateral obligations without losses. Insolvency occurs when an institution does not have sufficient assets to pay its debts. For example, an individual can own an expensive house but not have enough cash to pay this month's bills. Selling the house would take too long—hence, the owner is solvent but also illiquid. Same thing with banks.

As it now stands, economists generally agree that Shadow Banking does not threaten the liquidity of the entire Chinese banking system—but certain parts are quite vulnerable.

In one analysis of the risks of Shadow Banking on China's financial system, Jianjun Li and Sara Hsu conclude that the banks would survive a crisis. They ponder the impact of solvency and liquidity in Shadow Banking. As Li and Hsu note, "Liquidity appears to be adequate for the top five significant financial institutions but inadequate for the banking sector as a whole. Although the central government may stand by ready to inject funds into the banking sector where needed, it would be more efficient to ensure that banks are liquid before a credit crunch ensues, particularly since it may be more difficult to identify flagging banks in a crisis" (Li and Hsu 2013).

Others believe that liquidity may be a problem—but it is likely that the banks will be able to withstand a crisis. According to a report by the Brookings Institution, the banking system has adequate liquidity mainly due to the high levels of deposits from households and businesses, and reliance on fragile wholesale funding sources is minimal (which is what hurt the USA during the mortgage meltdown). "Bad events such as a property market crash, a dramatic heavy-industry slowdown, or defaults in the trust companies would certainly increase banks' non-performing assets, but they would not imperil banks' funding" (Elliott et al. 2015).

However, the growth of Shadow Banking in China has been much faster than in other countries—which means the risks may rise over time. The exchange rate-adjusted growth rate reached 30 percent and above in 2014 in Argentina and China, while other countries were generally below 10 percent. China rose from 1.6 percent of the global total in 2010 to 7.7 percent in 2014. This growth itself is a source of concern.

Share of Shadow Banking assets by country

	At end-2010	At end-2014
United States	40.9	39.7
United Kingdom	13.0	11.4
China	1.6	7.7
Ireland	6.9	7.6
Germany	7.1	7.2
Japan	9.5	6.8
France	6.1	4.4
Canada	2.4	2.8
Brazil	2.0	1.9
Korea	1.3	1.8

Source: Financial Stability Board

On the other hand, as a percentage of GDP, China's Shadow Banking assets are lower than in other countries. China ranks number 17 in the world, with 55 percent of GDP, including both Shadow Banks and other non-bank institutions like insurance companies, according to FSB data. (This data excludes certain categories of financing that could be considered Shadow Loans.)

Shadow Banking, other financial intermediaries, and banks as a percentage of GDP 26 jurisdictions at the end of 2014

	Shadow banking	OFIs	Total	Banks
Ireland	1190	1551	2741	363
Netherlands	74	838	912	326
United Kingdom	147	326	473	601
Switzerland	90	277	367	364
United States	82	148	230	122
Canada	58	147	205	228
France	61	96	156	370
Germany	73	81	154	241
Korea	48	100	148	205
Japan	60	87	147	374
Hong Kong	20	85	105	817
Singapore	10	90	101	607
Brazil	33	60	93	91
Australia	27	64	91	211
Spain	21	69	89	267

(*continued*)

(continued)

	Shadow banking	OFIs	Total	Banks
South Africa	27	61	88	108
China	26	29	55	271
Italy	17	38	55	223
Chile	23	31	54	106
Mexico	16	23	38	40

Source: Financial Stability Board (2015b)

Of course, Shadow Banking adds a layer of complexity to the financial system because it is not as well-regulated as other financial intermediations. Shadow Banking is non-transparent, is intimately connected to the financial system through many different products including WMPs and bonds, and most Shadow Banking institutions have high debt levels with little equity (Liao et al. 2016c).

The related question is China' ability to handle debt in general, including both the formal and informal banking system. In 2015, the IMF attempted to answer this question by looking at the financial health of China's corporate borrowers, who had the lion's share of the debt.

According to their analysis, considering estimates of bank loans potentially at risk and assuming a 60 percent loss ratio, suggests that potential bank losses on these loans could amount to $756 billion (7 percent of GDP). Assuming a lower loss ratio of 45 percent—a Basel II norm for defaulted loans—yields potential bank losses of $567 billion, or 5 percent of GDP.

They estimated that potential losses on loans at risk are substantial, but they are manageable given existing bank and policy buffers and the continued strong underlying growth in the economy. Estimated losses are equivalent to around 1.9 years of projected banking system pretax profits for 2015. Bank Tier 1 capital totals about $1.7 trillion, or11.3 percent of system risk-weighted assets, and bank reserves are $356 billion. Beyond bank buffers, China's public debt level—at 43 percent of GDP in 2015—provided space to address current estimates of potential bank losses (Global Stability Report 2015).

***

Another way of looking at Shadow Banking risks is to examine overall credit growth. Economists generally have utilized four metrics. These are:

1) The private sector credit-to-GDP ratio, which looks at the total amount of bank and non-bank credit to the private sector relative to GDP.
2) The growth of real credit per capita. In line with theories of financial development, credit per capita should increase as a country grows richer. Advanced economies display higher levels of credit per capita than developing countries. However, if the growth rate of credit relative to per capita income grows too rapidly, it can be a warning indicator of excessive credit growth. A credit boom is identified by credit growth of 1.75 times the standard deviation of the long- run trend. Applying this methodology to China reveals that a significant credit boom occurred in 1997 and lasted until the year 1999 (See Tables in page 151). The real credit per capita income gap in 2009 peaked just below the cutoff for a credit boom but has remained elevated for the last four years.
3) Similar to real credit per capita gap method, the real credit growth gap calculates the long-term trend of log real credit growth and then measures significant deviations (gaps) from that trend. This measurement, however, excludes any denominator and simply looks at the growth of credit itself. Using this method to analyze China produces virtually identical results to the real credit per capita gap method. There was a boom in credit in 1997, which lasted until 1999. Credit growth in 2009 came in just below the cutoff for a credit boom but has remained elevated for the past four years.
4) The debt service ratio method looks not at the aggregate amount of credit but at the expense associated with servicing existing debt. The debt service ratio for most of the 1990s and 2000s was around 20 percent, relatively high but stable. The postcrisis period shows a sharp uptick in the debt service ratio, from 21 percent at the end of 2008 to 33 percent by the first half of 2013, and has continued to grow.

None of these measures of credit suggest China is in good shape. "This analysis implies that China should be actively creating such a capital buffer in anticipation of future financial risks" (Borst 2013).

***

THE BALANCE SHEET ARGUMENT

One of the arguments made by Chinese economists is that China has plenty of money to pay off its debts and could easily avert a financial collapse. The government, they say, could function as lender of last resort. But what happens in a severe downturn may not conform to prior predictions. How does one confirm whether there are sufficient resources in China to provide adequate capital for a massive collapse in economic activity?

One useful way to test whether there is enough money to cover a collapse is to look at China's sovereign balance sheet. Just as a company has assets and liabilities, so do countries. This analysis is not as easy to calculate as with a company, because a country covers a lot more ground. But with the right tools, it can be a useful exercise. It also lays bare China's economy.

The real question is—can China use its resources in a time of crisis? If China suffers a financial meltdown can the government pay? Could China handle the so-called Minsky Moment when asset values collapse following a speculative bubble. The Minsky Moment is a term coined by PIMCO's (Pacific Investment Management Company) Paul McCulley about the 1998 Russian Financial Crisis, referring to the eclectic economist, Hyman Minsky.

One way to do this is to utilize a balance sheet for China compiled for the International Monetary Fund by economists Yang Li and Xiaojing Zhang. Their chart for 2010 shows total assets of 142.3 trillion renminbi and liabilities of 72.7 trillion renminbi, for total net worth of 69.6 trillion renminbi (Das et al. 2013).

Some items have changed since 2010. Both local government debt and overall bad loans are higher than their estimates given the passage of time but the overall analysis remains intact.

On the asset side, clearly the easiest source of usable capital is China's $3.3 trillion of foreign reserves. However, pulling them out of Western markets (mainly Europe and the USA) would send a strong negative signal and cause a decline in their value. The same applies to holdings of stocks; selling large amounts of shares in European banks would cause their value to plummet. Plus, importing foreign exchange would require massive sterilization by the PBOC—a process dubbed "mopping up"—by selling bonds and thus avoiding an inflationary spiral. So the reserves, while important, bring their own problems.

The next potential pool is China's 70 trillion renminbi in state assets. Many Chinese point to their state firms as a source of ready capital. Why not sell them off?

Easier said than done. There are 117,000 state firms in China with assets of 85 trillion renminbi. Beijing controls 106, while the remaining 116,000 are owned by Provincial governments. China is unlikely to sell off its most attractive firms. These are the Beijing-controlled state champions like its oil, nuclear, and electricity companies. That leaves the provincial state firms as a source of ready capital. But selling them is likely to be a difficult process. Combined, they employ 64 million people, a politically potent cohort. By industry, 30 percent of state firm investment is in manufacturing and 22 percent in real estate—two areas that are unlikely to be attractive to buyers. (Many of the manufacturing firms are in inefficient heavy industries like steel, for example, which would find few buyers.)

The other big asset on the country's balance sheet is 44.3 trillion in land (likely higher by now). On the face of it, this looks marketable. In 2013 alone, revenue from land sales rose 52.4 percent to more than 4 trillion renminbi, although it declined in subsequent years. But tapping into land sales to pay for systemic debts is problematic for two reasons. First, local governments are slowly running out of land; second, if China is faced with a fiscal crisis it is highly likely that property values will collapse like a punctured bicycle tire, thus deflating land prices.

There are other sources of capital, such as savings deposits in the banks that could be used to prop up the financial system. But using these savings would be a measure of last resort. China's balance sheet, as with many countries in an economic downturn, may not be that helpful in turning the tide. Unalloyed faith in China's balance sheet is a bit like a circus acrobat who fails to test his safety net until it's too late.

* * *

There are a number of other, more specific concerns both about Shadow Banking in China. One of these are the Trusts.

Trusts are the weakest link in the Shadow Banking food chain. That is because (1) they have few assets compared with the loans they make, and (2) they work closely with the banks who are at the center of China's financial system. As Li and Hsu note, "From 2007 to 2012, the Trust company was the most powerful engine for systemic risk...two factors likely contribute to this development. One factor is that the asset-liability ratio of Trust companies was low in recent years, leading to risk contagion from assets to liabilities. The other is that Trust companies depend greatly on cooperation with other institutions, especially banks, concentrating the distribution of debtors. So the risk within Trust companies tended to spill over" (Li and Hsu 2014).

Earlier, in the section on Trusts, we discussed the collapse of a loan called Credit Equals Gold. Credit Equals Gold may have been among the most flagrant abuses of the Trusts, but it was not the only one. The rapid rise of credit that flowed through the Trusts made them ripe for bad loans. As we closely watched the growth of the Trust industry post-stimulus, red flags began popping up.

First of all, the Trusts were shoveling loans out the door as quickly as they could. In 2014, according to our own analysis, the industry started to issue fewer financial investment products but there was a significant increase in capital per product sold. Instead of carefully matching loans with borrowers, it was easier for the Trusts to collect funds from a number of wealthy individuals and then find a borrower. As oversight declined, this "bulk packaging" of Trust products added even more risk to the industry.

The Financial Stability Board, a global banking regulator, compiled international data about Shadow Banks, which they refer to as other financial intermediaries (OFI). And they warn of the dangers of Chinese Trusts.

Globally, Shadow Banking assets have become larger, reaching 128 percent of assets in 2014 for the average large country (both emerging and advanced nations), up from 122 percent in 2013. In particular, the sophistication of financial markets within the larger, Western nations has resulted in larger Shadow Banking assets. The Financial Stability Board (FSB) notes that Shadow Banking in 2014 was largest in Europe ($29 trillion), the USA ($26 trillion), and the United Kingdom ($9 trillion). These nations accounted for 80 percent of Shadow Banking assets globally.

In the West, where the lion's share of Shadow Banking assets are, most reside in investment funds, which accounted for $27 trillion or 40 percent of global Shadow Banking assets. A little more than half of the funds were allocated to equity funds ($14.1 trillion), followed by fixed income funds ($9.1 trillion) and other funds ($4.2 trillion).

The contrast with China is striking. Where the Western financial markets created giant pools of Shadow Capital tossed between financial intermediaries like boats in a stormy sea, China's Shadow Banking assets were concentrated in Shadow Banks. The biggest of these were the Trusts. The FSB notes that global Trust companies' assets rose to $2.7 trillion in 2014, with their share of Shadow Banking rising to 4 percent in 2014 from 3 percent in 2013. Most of this increase occurred in China. Within China, Trust companies' assets, as a share of Chinese

GDP, reached 22 percent in 2014, from 8 percent in 2010. "Given the fast growth in sector assets, a careful monitoring of potential risk build-up is warranted," the FSB warned (Financial Stability Board 2015).

There are other hidden risks in the Trust investments. One has been the network of linkages; the products don't exist on their own but often were interconnected with different parties and geographic regions. These links often took the form of guarantees from a number of different parties.

Usually, when a bank makes a loan, it relies on collateral such as the value of a house for a mortgage. For a corporation, it might be machinery. However, Trusts relied not on assets but on guarantees. These could come from a government (technically illegal), a company, another Trust, or a specific guarantee company. Collateral often was secondary.

We looked at a number of Trust products to analyze what was behind the loan. In most cases, it was either collateral or a vaguely defined "guarantee."

Guarantees are a particularly Chinese form of financial management. They exist in the West, as when a parent guarantees a student loan. But they tend not to be utilized for entire industrial or infrastructure projects; there's too much risk and uncertainty about the viability of the guarantor. But in China, guarantees are common. The guarantees behind the Trust products were a confused mess. Each Trust product had its own set of opaque guarantors—none of which made much sense. These included complicated cross guarantees between different corporate and government entities.

For guarantees, the hardest part of the analysis was understanding the language of prospectuses, which often was purposefully confusing. For example, the Zhongyuan Trust 314 Capital Trust guarantor "guarantees strength and relatively good qualities." Others are so complicated it's not clear who's doing what to whom. The Hefei "Spring Lake SME loan collection Feixi Trust" states "Hefei Xingtai financing will be invited to provide a joint liability guarantee with the guarantee control rate less than 2 per cent." Most worrying—and further muddying the picture—was the existence of several different entities—companies, governments, Trusts—providing guarantees, whose relationships were not clearly spelled out. And this wasn't the result of bad translation; the original Chinese is equally confusing.

In an analysis of the collateral behind 20 Trust products, what we found was disturbing. In most cases, the collateral had little value. About one-third of the collateral consisted of company shares, 23 percent were based on land, 17 percent were guarantees, while 23 percent didn't appear to have any collateral whatsoever. There was also a small category for "other" which included accounts receivables, or money owed for goods or services delivered.

The use of company shares as collateral was a lot more frequent than we had suspected. This included both traded and non-traded shares (which are basically just a private investment in a company). Frequently, their value was not stated, nor were underlying financials provided. Company shares that are not traded on an exchange are very difficult to value and are virtually worthless as collateral. For example, the Xu Hui Shanghai Cambridge project Stock Right Investment Trust Collection Plan Trust stated that one investor, Radiant Group, was providing 50 percent of its shares in the targeted Trust investment project as collateral. Imagine using shares in an unfinished construction as collateral for itself! Also, land was a frequently used form of collateral. Land does have value, but it is necessary to have an independent assessment of the value of the land which was not included in any documents we saw.

WHAT GOVERNMENT?

The reason that there is often a very careless provision for guarantees or collateral is that lenders assume that there is a government standing somewhere behind the loan. But what government? Shadow Banking in all forms, particularly during the stimulus boom, blurred the line between the market and the state. Suddenly, all sorts of institutions were claiming to be owned, partly owned, or vaguely connected with the government. And they were providing guarantees based on these unclear links with local governments.

Let's take a look at this confused hodgepodge of agreements in a single Trust product: the Helen Growing Collection of Real Estate Trust Fund Plan, issued by Zhongrong Trust. The Trust was part of a 2.9 billion renminbi Yanta City residential real estate development in the eastern suburbs of Xian, a large city in Western China famous for the Terra Cotta Warriors. Who was backing the loan in case of failure?

First, there was an entity called the Guangdong Yi Investment Group. We generally assume that investment groups are just another name for LGFVs—basically government-backed companies. Guangdong Yi provided a joint liability guarantee. In addition, the borrowers of the money pledged their shares in three companies as collateral: the Fort Guangdong Helen Real Estate Group, Guangzhou City Fan Sau Venture Capital, and the Xian

De Maoxing Company. However, there was no description in the Trust product about what these companies did or how profitable they were.

So what happens if the loan were to fail? It's unlikely the property developer itself would have the cash as they tend to be cash short, particularly when they are in the middle of construction. The Trust itself, Zhongrong, is a likely candidate for a government bailout. It is a large and powerful Beijing-based Trust, with 2013 profits of 2.7 billion renminbi. It also had a joint venture with State Street in Boston, a large investment fund, which may have added to its reputation. The problem is that Zhongrong and other Trusts generally don't have much capital. In 2015, on average, the Chinese Trusts had only 2 percent in equity supporting their outstanding investments. In other words, *for every 1 billion renminbi in investments, the average Trust only had 20 million renminbi in capital to back them up.* Hardly enough for a minor default, let alone a financial crisis. That's precisely why they are Trusts and not banks. Banks have to keep a certain amount of reserves on hand for their loans. Trusts don't, because technically they are not making loans but merely arranging investments.

So, despite all these guarantees, there really was no clear group behind the Helen Growing Collection. In case of a default, it's unlikely any of these various Guangdong groups would foot the bill. We really can't say whether these groups are real private companies, or just shell companies for the Guangdong Government. Either way, why would a Guangdong LGFV bail out a property development in Xian, hundreds of miles away in Shaanxi province?

We now have a case of interprovincial politics. A failed residential development in the city of Xian in Shaanxi province could become the liability of the Guangdong government.

We also examined data on the few Trusts that had defaulted or came close to default. Generally, governments hide the failure of a loan by convincing a bank to supply new loans or by forcing a local company to buy the bad assets. In most cases, the issuers of the Trust products are reluctant to discuss the collapse of their projects. We were able to collect data on the reason for the defaults on 13 Trust products. The majority of this group suffered from a category we call "weak sales." This is a catch-all term to describe a poor project that was unprofitable—basically, failed investments. Low coal prices, bad management, and misuse of funds each were cited in six other cases.

We also examined the outcome of the defaults. We were surprised to note that liquidation was the most popular exit vehicle. Because almost 90 percent of the 67 Trusts were owned by provincial or central governments, we had assumed they would step in to recapitalize any failing products they sold. Of this group:

1) Twelve of the 31 Trusts were liquidated outright. We assumed this included the sale of existing assets, but as most investments were likely in uneconomic property projects, it is doubtful much capital was recovered.
2) In four of the 31, the Trusts did step in to pay off investors, probably concerned about the reputational risk of having a failed Trust on their hands.
3) In three cases, collateral was sold to pay off investors—which is how most loans are supposed to function in case of a default.
4) In three cases, payment was delayed, so the actual workout was still in question. Two were in litigation at the time of writing and two were transferred to other financial entities, another form of juggling debt between financial groups. Often these financial firms are related and are merely passing bad assets back and forth.

The bottom line? The Trusts are a perfect example of how shaky financials are fine when things are going well—but can become a disaster in a downturn. And the vast network of linkages through collateral and guarantees doesn't provide much assurance.

Can the courts handle these disputes in the Shadow Banking market? The courts are trying to—but look like they are becoming overwhelmed. According to President of the Supreme People's Court (SPC) Zhou Qiang's March 2015 report to the National People's Congress, in 2014 Chinese courts heard over one million Shadow Banking disputes, accounting for 20 percent of all civil cases in the Chinese courts. Putting together that data with a more recently released report on data concerning civil and commercial cases, Shadow Banking disputes constituted about 60 percent of all loan disputes heard in the Chinese courts. Zhejiang, nationally known for its active private business sector, led the way with 132,000 cases in 2014 (110,000 in 2013), of which about 15,000 were heard in the Wenzhou courts, with total amounts in dispute of over 86.3. billion renminbi. A report by a Qingdao city court published at the end of 2015 noted that private lending cases accounted for about half of commercial cases, and the amounts of disputes and complexity were escalating (Finder 2015).

We do note that the regulators over time improved their control over the Trusts. In 2010, the CBRC instituted a rule mandating that Trust firms must hold net capital of at least 200 million renminbi or 40 percent of net assets, whichever is greater. Trusts had 12 months to meet the new requirement. Then, in 2016, the CBRC issued the draft of guidelines on the rating and classified regulation of Trust companies (Xueqing 2014). They then became rated according to six criteria, including risk, management of assets, and other factors. In addition, they had to either restrict their businesses and reduce net assets or have shareholders replenish capital when the firms suffer losses.

However, as late as the spring of 2015, just before the Chinese stock market crashed, Trusts poured money into "tradable instruments," which included stocks. While loans outstanding grew just 8 percent in 2014—far below the 62 percent growth in 2013—growth in obscure asset categories including "tradable financial assets" and "saleable fixed-term investments" was 77 percent and 47 percent, respectively (Taplin 2015).

By redirecting money into capital markets and OTC products like asset-backed securities and bankers' acceptances, Trusts continued to act less like regulated banks and more like hedge funds or lightly regulated mutual funds.

∗ ∗ ∗

Weak Local Banks

Earlier, in our discussion of WMPs, we touched briefly on the role of small banks in Shadow Banking. Smaller banks in China have a tougher time convincing savers and the better borrowers to use their services. Thus, the smaller banks are generally involved in riskier lending than their larger competitors.

The big SOE banks have a number of advantages. First, they enjoy implicit government guarantees on their bank loans. Second, large banks, being state-owned, are a primary funding source for state firms of strategic importance to the government, as in defense and energy. Third, large banks have a stable and deep relationship with households so that they encounter little difficulty in acquiring additional deposits to overcome unexpected deposit shortfalls. The small banks don't have these advantages.

In addition, when faced with lending restriction such as the mandatory ratios between deposits and loans, small banks are under greater pressure to find new sources of profits. The end result has been more risky Shadow Banking lending. Efforts to clamp down on risky lending just made things worse for the small banks as they searched for ways to obtain capital.

"Our study demonstrates that these well-intended regulations had an unintended consequence: they encouraged Chinese small banks to bring supposed off-balance-sheet risks into on-balance-sheet risks during the period of monetary tightening through the means of risky entrusted lending" (Chen et al 2016).

More broadly, smaller banks, particularly the smaller city and rural banks, tend to be concentrated in fiscally weaker parts of the country. This is a big risk in a downturn. In the city of Jinzhou, Liaoning province, population 810,000, the market share of the larger state banks is only 19.4 percent, while the local Bank of Jinzhou has a share of 62.6 percent. A weakening property market would devastate the bank (IPO Prospectus, Bank of Jinzhou). In a time of crisis, the bank would be further weakened by its exposure to Shadow Banking. In 2015, it had 30.6 billion renminbi of WMPs, or 9.8 percent of its total assets. Technically, a default of these WMPs wouldn't be the bank's problem, since they are off-balance sheet financial instruments. But the local customers might see it differently, causing a run on the bank.

One of the predictors for the success or failure of a country's banking system is how effective it is at distributing risk. Banks that are concentrated in distinct geographic areas isolated from each other are unable to distribute capital in times of crisis. The USA's federalist structure, where states have been separate legal entities with their own laws, also prevented banks from consolidating nationally. This economic isolation resulted in far more bank failures than in many other countries.

Because of this geographic and legislative separation, the USA has had a weak banking system:

"The United States has had 14 banking crises over the past 180 years! Canada, which shares not only a 2,000-mile border with the United States but also a common culture and language, had only two brief and mild bank illiquidity crises during the same period, in 1837 and 1839, neither of which involved significant bank failures. Since that time, some Canadian banks have failed, but the country has experienced no systemic banking crises. The Canadian banking system has been extraordinarily stable—so stable, in fact, that there has been little need for government intervention in support of the banks since Canada became an independent country in 1867." Ibid, *Fragile By Design*, p. 5

In China, the state banks spread their risk nationally. There are 213,000 bank branches in China. The Bank of China alone has 10,691 branches.

Combined with the other state banks, they have in total more than 50,000 branches, or about 25 percent share. The local banks are thus more vulnerable. Any weakness in the Chinese economy, such as a collapsing property bubble, will hit certain regions more than others—and the banks there, too.

***

Collapsing Property Bubble The property market is important for China's economy in general. But it is crucial for China's Shadow Banking. Many of the products sold to investors raised money for property projects. Eight years after the stimulus there has been a rising tide of defaults. According to research by Susan Finder, Visiting Lecturer at the School of Transnational Law of Peking University in Shenzhen, and an expert on China's legal system, the disputes include:

- **Disputes over Land Grants.** In 2015, these disputes rose 21 percent to 1,368.
- **Disputes over Real Estate Sales.** Up 43 percent to 172,372 involving the sale by real estate developers. Problems include poor government oversight of developers (because the local government is desperate for investment); developers pre-selling real estate development projects although their rights to the land are in dispute; poor quality building, misleading sales advertising, and cases involving large numbers of litigants.
- **Arguments over Joint Ventures.** These cases, where one company provides the capital and the other the land, rose 20 percent to 1946. Some cases involve deals between state-owned companies from different provinces, with the out-of-town party often trying to move the case to a more favorable legal venue.

In 2015, the Supreme People's Court identified the following problems in real estate development cases:

- Developers suing to invalidate grant contracts (under which they purchase land for development) and seek the return of the land grant fees (upon which local governments depend);
- Developers who are short of funds and unable to hand over properties on time;
- Declines in property prices causing "mass incidents";

- Cases involving real estate development and private lending, including illegal fund-raising;
- Many cases involving unpaid migrant construction workers.

The Court said it expected an increase in real estate development companies going into bankruptcy. These bankruptcies would have a significant impact on the country's capital structure—including Shadow Banking. Local governments would lose revenue from land sales and real estate fees, and developers would be unable to pay back loans supplied by the Trusts, bank WMPs, and other private sources (Finder 2016).

Beyond the legal issues, the concentration of Shadow Loans to the property sector is worrisome. The data is not terribly clear, as we have noted earlier, due to what we believe is bad reporting by local governments.

In 2013, The National Audit Office estimated that 43.4 percent of local debt was borrowed from non-banks. Bonds may have been around 10 percent, but the majority—or about one-third—of all local loans were from the Shadow Banks. Much of this was lent to property developers. This capital that helped fuel the property bubble could just as easily be withdrawn. Most of it is short-term, anywhere from two years to as little as overnight. Thus, this maturity mismatch—short-term loans for long-term projects—is a huge risk to the Chinese economy, and particularly where a property bubble has already started to deflate.

***

As we have noted earlier, Beijing has not been blind to the rampant rise of Shadow Banking. The first step was to attempt to collect data on the size of the sector and where the lending was occurring. One of the most important regulatory steps was a series of surveys conducted by the National Audit Office of the debt held by the provinces and the cities and townships within them. These local debt audits occurred in 2011 and 2013 and gave authorities some sense of the scope of the problem.

Other significant changes occurred. Once the growth of WMPs became noticeable, the PBOC stepped in with new methods for calculating these Shadow Banking flows from private citizens. These included information on the transactions, the transaction dates, term structures, counter-parties, interest rates, and other factors (Qizheng 2013).

Later, in 2014, the State Council issued Document Number 107 to specify which kinds of Shadow Banking should be subject to regulation.

There were three categories: unlicensed and unregulated, unlicensed and lightly regulated, and licensed but insufficiently regulated. Although the goal was to clamp down on rampant credit creation by virtually rogue groups, the document had holes large enough to drive a truck through. A later notice, No. 127, had more firepower, mainly because the PBOC, the CBRC, and three other financial regulators got together to issue new regulations (Tsai, Political Economy, p. 21).

In 2016, the Shanghai branch of the regulator in charge of approving new business applications—the State Administration for Industry and Commerce, or SAIC—told agents in the city who handle those applications that it will refuse those that seem investment-related. The new rules followed the arrest of 21 executives of a high-profile local investment business for suspected illegal fund-raising, and a demand by the Shanghai government that the SAIC improve oversight (Wall Street Journal 2016)

This was caused by a flood of new financial products luring unsuspecting investors.

Z-Ben Advisors, a Shanghai-based consulting firm, counted about 160,000 investment products—for everything from private equity funds to typical mutual funds to bank trust products—at the end of 2015, a 30 percent jump from 2014. The new rules forced banks to stop using wealth management funds to invest directly or indirectly in their own investment products. The lenders would also have to fully provision for the investment products that are based on bank loans. (FT story, May 2016, China Financial Regulator).

But the CBRC and the PBOC have generally been a step or two behind the banks and others in the market. One huge growth in credit occurred with investment funds, rising from 6 trillion renminbi in January 2015 to more than 12 trillion renminbi by the end of the year. These weren't Shadow funds per se—they were investments by the banks—but the liquidity they provided helped fuel Shadow Banking. And they often were funded by WMPs, which is a type of Shadow Lending. It wasn't until June 2016 that the CBRC finally forced the banks to consider these like loans with the same risk controls.

***

There are some who are more optimistic. They believe Shadow Banking offers a way forward for the Chinese economy. "I believe Shadow Banking has a very valuable, social and economic function a modern financial system," noted Fred Hu, a former Goldman Sachs Director who now runs his own lending firm in China. He called it a natural development of financial deepening of China's economy. Financial repression caused a loss of income to savers that threatened their livelihood and retirement. Too many loans were made to corporates and not consumers. Shadow Banking has changed that (Hu 2015).

However, at the same panel discussion, the former chairman of the CBRC warned that, unless it was constrained, Shadow Banking could cause significant problems. "The most important thing is the interconnectedness between Shadow Banking and the traditional banks. By the end of the day, it could cause a huge stir in terms of social unrest." Ibid, Panel Discussion. Liu Mingkang.

The Asia Global Institute, formerly called the Fung Global Institute, published a report in 2015 that took a positive view on Shadow Banking. They made four substantive points:

1) China's national balance sheet is positive.
2) China has low household debt and is not facing a mortgage crisis.
3) Concerns over fast-rising corporate debt/GDP ratio are inflated, mainly because corporations put cash on deposit, a practice not used elsewhere in the world.
4) China is a net lender to the rest of the world and is therefore not prone to global issues.

As noted above, the key issue is whether the assets can be sold. Three cannot be easily liquidated. China's $3 trillion plus in foreign exchange cannot be disposed of without consequences for the value of the assets. The same holds for China's 70 trillion renminbi in state assets and 44 trillion renminbi in land. China's aging industrial plants and the increasingly less valuable land on city outskirts would be difficult to sell, particularly if the country were to undergo a sharp downturn.

The third point about corporate debt is not convincing, either. Even Ma Jun, chief economist of the PBOC, has said that China's corporate debt, at more than 150 percent of GDP, is high by international standards.

The last point is accurate, however. The disconnect between China's financial markets and the rest of the world due to its closed financial account insulates it from the kind of rapid flows of capital that led to the Asian Financial Crisis.

Others have noted the benefits of Shadow Banking. According to a report by the IMF:

- It contributes to developing the capital market and reduces over-reliance on the banking system.
- It helps diversify risks in banking sector.
- It provides incentives for financial reform. For example, the funding cost in trust loans and underground lending in China seem to have reflected market demand and supply, and WMPs are an effective way to circumvent the control on deposit rates (similar to the CD market in the USA under Regulation Q).
- Shadow banking has helped temporarily relieve the liquidity shortage of the financial system.

We agree with these points and have particularly stressed the third point about financial reform and the benefits for small business and capitalism in general. The question is how to balance these advantages over the risks (Liao et al. 2016a).

∗∗∗

At bottom, the fundamental concern about Shadow Banking in China goes to the heart of China's political and economic system. The principal problem is not overly complicated financial products. The biggest worry is moral hazard. This refers to risk taken by one party where that party is not responsible for the potential cost. The classic example is a car owner who buys theft insurance and then doesn't safeguard his belongings; she figures the insurance company will cover the cost.

For China, the difficulty is figuring out who's covered by insurance—or in China's case, the state. The state is a potential financial backer for every part of the economy. Beijing's almost purposeful confusion about what is government backed and what is not encourages the country's financial actors, and the general population, to assume that the state will support every part of the economy—even if in a crisis it won't. Lenders—banks, non-banks, or private individuals—often feel free to lend, knowing they may not have to bear the costs of a default. Surely Beijing would step in if things went sour?

For example, a bank may arrange the sale of a WMP knowing that it is not responsible for a bad loan because it is "off-balance sheet." That means it isn't the bank's responsibility. Meanwhile, the buyer of the financial product may assume that the bank will support the loan, because she bought it there. In the worst case, the government would backstop the bank. After all, it's a state-owned bank, isn't it?

The real problem is the lack of a clear line between the state and private activity. This is particularly true of Shadow Banks. Shadow Loans can be arranged by a government-owned Trust, a state-owned bank, a private bank, or a group of private lenders. When a state-owned bank arranges a loan from a wealthy person to a property project, is this a private or a state transaction? Is the Bank behind the loan or not? What if the property project is partly controlled by an LGFV? Are LGFVs private firms (as the CBRC defines them), or does the government stake (usually in the form of land) make them state entities (as the banks implicitly classify them?) We have touched on this theme earlier in the book. Given the complexity, it is difficult to resolve this question in these pages.

At the time of writing there had yet to be a widespread financial crisis as a result of Shadow Banking; the dominos had yet to fall. However, it is questionable whether Beijing would be able to protect all lenders during a widespread financial panic. What happens if there is? Who would be responsible?

One way to consider this question is to look at a single sector: mortgage loans. Chinese analysts often argue that China cannot undergo a financial crisis because, unlike the USA, mortgages are a small part of the economy and there is virtually no mortgage securitization market that could go haywire. The systemic problems that led to the US financial crisis just don't exist in China, in their view. The US Financial crisis in 2008 was in part caused by a huge pool of capital controlled by investment banks and retirement funds that spun out of control through the creation of fancy derivative products with little regulatory oversight. China doesn't have a huge pension system, and its financial markets make up only a small fraction of total economic activity. Therefore, a mortgage crisis is unlikely.

We recently heard this argument from a former PBOC official in Guangzhou. China's debt is not "systemic" in the way the US debt was, and China has more than adequate resources (including foreign exchange and bank savings) to handle a financial crisis. UBS economist Wang Tao agrees. China's Shadow Banking is manageable because of the "lack of leverage and securitization, and mark-to-market mechanism in China's shadow banking system" (Tao 2014.).

Mortgages are definitely lower in China. They are about 15 percent of GDP in China compared with 80 percent in the USA. Total household debt is around 10 percent of GDP compared with 120 percent in the USA. Also, there is virtually no securitization of mortgages in China, so the vast linkages between traded financial products and the banking system itself that led to the US mortgage crisis don't exist in China.

However, leaving aside the formal "financialization" of the economy, there are more *informal* risks relating to the connections between Shadow Banking products we outlined earlier. A private citizen can make a loan through a WMP for property construction across the country. He is putting his faith in a project about which he knows very little—and the bank that arranged the WMP has not examined in detail, either, because it is not the bank's responsibility. A dispute over a project could easily involve a host of participants: private citizens, provincial Trusts, local banks, LGFVs, and state banks. In the end, it is highly likely (and the few cases that we have seen) everyone will turn to the largest state institution that is involved and expect them to solve the problem. That institution may step in—probably a state-owned bank—but it is also likely a lot of participants in the lengthy chain of capital will get hurt. The risks of Shadow Banking are less *systemic* than they will be specific to individuals, geographies, and institutions. Who gets hurt and who doesn't is the more important question.

Thus, the issue of moral hazard will become fundamental to the future of Shadow Banking. This will be trench warfare. China's inability to define the edges of the state will haunt the country as economic growth slows, debt overwhelms the economy, and Shadow Banking loans start to default. It's going to be a messy political fight.

CHAPTER 11

What Does the Future Hold for Shadow Banking?

Walk through the side streets of Beijing, under the watchful eye of towering buildings like the China Central Television tower and the 83-story China World Trade Center, and you will happen upon a woman, busy slapping dough into pancakes to fashion a local delicacy called Jian Bing. It's a kind of a pancake topped with a spicy sauce. When my children were young they would paddle out to the street in their pajamas and buy them for breakfast, slurping them down like McDonald's hamburgers. These entrepreneurs usually borrow money from family members, purchase a gas stove, rent a tiny storefront, and start frying. That money is a Shadow Loan. The woman is a fledgling capitalist.

In this book we have been discussing a much larger group of institutions that supply Shadow Loans. And much larger businesses that receive them. But the point is that private business, from the Jian Bing seller to giant property companies, have benefited from the allocation of capital by the Shadow Banks. Of course, the Shadow Banks have also provided loans to inefficient and capital-wasting institutions that are not capitalist enterprises. Given these disparate forces, what is the future of Shadow Banking and its relationship to capitalism in China?

To answer this, we will address two issues: first, how—and to what degree—Shadow Banking has fostered capitalism. And second, how will China's slowing economy affect Shadow Banking?

***

© The Author(s) 2017

A. Collier, *Shadow Banking and the Rise of Capitalism in China*, DOI 10.1007/978-981-10-2996-7_11

There is one large recipient of Shadow Banking loans that is difficult to categorize as a private or state enterprise: LGFVs. As discussed earlier, these hybrid firms generally borrowed money from state banks, local banks, Shadow Banks, and entrepreneurs. Can we use them as evidence of rising capitalism in China?

LGFVs have strong government support, which would appear to exclude them from being categorized as companies operating under a market structure. Local governments' financial position is often included as one criterion used by banks to assess the creditworthiness of LGFVs, along with other factors such as central government policies toward certain sectors in which the LGFVs may conduct business. This occurs even though these local governments are legally not allowed to guarantee loans to LGFVs. In addition, most LGFVs begin business with government support in the form of land, a hugely important subsidy.

It's also likely that these firms fall short in one obvious measure of capitalism: profits. First of all, their interest burden is quite high due to the debt incurred during their launch. The IMF estimates that, in 2011, the LGFVs' 4.97 trillion renminbi of debt would have incurred interest payments of 320 billion renminbi, or about 6 percent of total local government revenue (Lu and Sun 2013).That's a significant interest burden for companies just getting off the ground. There is virtually no national data on the profitability of LGFV investments. They are purported to be infrastructure-related, meaning that they contribute to the underlying efficiency of the economy, but they aren't necessarily supposed to be profitable. As we discussed earlier, the numbers most likely understate the investment by LGFVs in the property sector. These investments in the property industry may have been profitable over the past decade during the boom years but overconstruction is likely to have dissipated many of the returns.

In addition, in 2015, Beijing launched a new program forcing state banks to exchange local government debt—most of which was incurred by the LGFVs—for local bonds. The interest rate for the bonds was not calculated according to any local metrics, such as local debt and revenue, but instead was set at the price of central government bonds. This suggests that even Beijing was treating local debt as a sovereign obligation. This is another sign that these firms are not really private.

So, the LGFVs are strong evidence for the misallocation of capital, from both formal and Shadow banks.

What will happen to the thousands of LGFVs across China? Given that most are likely wasting capital, most will be allowed to wither away, becoming failed projects like the One Thousand Tree Farm we visited in Yunnan province. However, others may gradually be weaned from subsidized loans from the banks and gradually will become efficient private business—launched with cheap capital and subsidized land—but morphing into capitalist enterprises. How many will survive and how many will die is difficult to tell. At that point, they will fall into another category closer to private enterprise.

* * *

The LGFVs may be examples of the misuse of Shadow loans. However, there have been more positive signs about the contribution of Shadow Banking to capitalism. Shadow Banking has created new investment channels for ordinary citizens. One way to look at this is to examine where Chinese allocate their savings. In the chapter on financial repression, we noted that Chinese citizens for decades were forced to put their money into the state-controlled banks for low returns because they had no alternatives. That was a windfall to the state-run system because the banks obtained low cost capital and could lend at higher rates. Shadow Banking, along with other financial reforms, has helped to open up new investment opportunities for ordinary citizens.

The data confirms this liberalization of investment alternatives. The chart below shows that Chinese citizens have gradually moved closer to the rest of the world in their investments. In 2016, Chinese investments in cash and deposits, at 45 percent, were only 10 percentage points below the global average. There are some differences between China and the rest of the world regarding allocation to insurance, pension, and investment funds, areas that are developing rapidly in China. However, purchases of company shares (stocks) at the time of the survey were almost the same, at 20 percent for China compared with 18 percent globally.

Chinese financial household allocation compared with global peers

	China	Global average
Other	NA	NA
Insurance and pension	9%	35%
Direct stocks	20%	18%
Investment funds/trusts	24%	6%
Bonds	NA	34%
Cash and deposits	45%	34%

Source: Citibank Research, 2016

The chart above does not break down how much of the capital was allocated through Shadow Banking channels such as WMPs and Trust products. We can assume, though, that the allocation includes such channels. We have also demonstrated that Shadow Banking increased pressure on the banks to offer new investment products with higher returns. This process is likely to continue both because of demand from customers, and interest among banks to continue to diversify their services, and is a favorable trend for efficient allocation of capital—Capitalism. We expect this liberalization to continue; Chinese have gotten used to these alternative investments, and borrowers need the funds. We see larger funds, better regulation, and a broader variety of financial tools in China's future. Shadow Banks helped to launch this trend.

***

On a hot spring day I was sitting in the office of a top executive with a Big Four state bank. As we sipped green tea, I asked him about the rising problem of bad loans. The official numbers at the time were quite low, hovering around 1.5 percent of all loans. However, very few people, both inside and outside, believed that. Instead, they assumed the bad loans could range anywhere from 5 percent to as much as 20 percent of the total.

My question was simple. Given all this credit that had exploded in China from both the Banks and the Shadow Banks, wasn't there also a boom in bad loans? The answer was yes. But surprisingly, it wasn't the state firms that were the problem. Everyone knew the state corporations were inefficient and squandered money right and left. So I assumed that's where the bad loans were. However, at least in Fujian province on the coast of China where this bank was located, it was the private entrepreneurs that had gone belly up. Apparently, they had greedily sucked down as much capital as they could get their hands on during the stimulus and post-stimulus period, and had gone to town with it—with disastrous results.

This raises the interesting question of whether Shadow Banking is good or bad for these entrepreneurs. Usually, the answer would be "good," because the Shadow Banks are an important source of loans to small businesses. That's certainly what happened in the early years of informal finance under Deng Xiaoping. But was it true more recently and has this been a good use of funds?

Why is this important? SMEs are the seeds of capitalism in China and a significant source of employment. SMEs account for 96 percent of registered enterprises in China; about 98 percent of China's SMEs are privately owned or controlled, employ 65 percent of the workforce, and generate 60 percent of China's GDP (Tsai 2016.)

***

In a mid-1990s survey of private entrepreneurs, nearly two-thirds used informal finance, and, in a 2012 survey of 15 provinces, 57.5 percent relied on informal finance.

The shortage of formal loans to SMEs is the result of four factors:

- A political ideology that puts a priority on supporting employment at state firms.
- An industrial policy that favors certain sectors over others, usually ones with significant state backing (such as telecommunications or energy).
- Financial repression, whereby lower interest rates to savers provides inexpensive capital to state firms.
- Limited organizational capacity to seek out and lend to SMEs.

Shadow Banking has been hugely helpful in providing credit to SMEs. As the chart below shows, the major Shadow Banks (excluding WMPs sold by banks and other institutions) devoted a substantial portion of their lending to SMEs—as much as three-quarters in the case of credit guarantee companies, which guarantee loans for a fee. There are 8000 credit guarantee firms in China.

Shadow Banking loans to SMEs in China

	Amount (Rmb trillion)	*% total*
Credit guarantee companies	1.69	75.8%
Micro-finance	0.93	39.0%
Trusts	16.58	38.9%
P2P	0.55	37.9%
Financial leasing companies	0.86	10.0%
Pawn shops	0.092	9.8%
Crowdfunding	0.067	NA
Rural credit coops	2.3	NA
	23.07	

Source: Tsai (2016)

From 1992 through 1999, retained earnings financed about 40–50 percent of the investment of all non-financial corporations in China. But from 2000 through 2008, this ratio rose to an average of 71 percent. The data for 1995 show that urban credit cooperatives supplied 80 percent of the formal credit flowing to private businesses, while the state banks' share had fallen to less than 20 percent. Lardy notes in *Markets Over Mao* that "historically state firms have borrowed about twice as much as private firms. Their share of outstanding loans at the end of 2009 was 56 per cent, more than twice the 26 per cent share of private firms. However, by 2012 private firms' share had increased by 10 percentage points, roughly mirroring a decline in the state firms' share" (*Markets Over Mao*, Location 2342, Kindle Edition).

***

The data does suggest that small businesses have had less access to capital than larger firms. Along with Sara Hsu of the State University of New York at New Paltz, one of the leading experts in Shadow Banking, I assembled data on SME access to capital to present at the 2014 Shadow Banking conference sponsored by the Central University of Finance and Economics. We used data originally collected by the Chinese Administration of Industry and Commerce, and the National Association of Industry and Commerce. The data was then assembled by the Chinese University of Hong Kong.

We asked three questions:

1) What were the funding risks to SMEs as the Chinese economy slows?
2) What sectors among SMEs had access to state capital and which sectors did not?
3) Did SME access to formal capital through the banks change after the financial crisis?

The data was from two periods: 4,000 firms in 2008 and another 5,097 firms in 2012. We calculated the ratio of non-bank loans to total loans. For 2008, the non-bank loans came from City Commercial Banks, Credit Unions, and non-regulated financial institutions. For 2012, the survey included non-regulated financial institutions. We picked 15 independent variables including the company's age, registered type, industry, and profit margin. We arrived at several conclusions:

1) Traditional state sectors automatically receive support from the banks. These included mining and manufacturing.
2) The banks also supplied capital to local governments through intermediary companies, suggesting the importance to local governments of land sales.
3) There was a surprising willingness of banks to consider lending to private growth tech sectors despite the risks.
4) Unwillingness by the state sector to invest in industries with the largest employment (e.g., retail).
5) A lack of support for agriculture, which ultimately could have negative effects on redistribution of income.

In 2013, the State Council came up with a plan to support loans to SMEs. They asked the banks to promote SME loans and requested the Ministry of Finance to provide additional policies in favor of local banks.

This study confirms what many had suspected: the SMEs in China relied heavily on credit from the informal sector of the economy. This is likely to continue due to the nature of the Chinese financial system and political structure.

***

Leaving aside the support for small business, there is a dark side to the future of Shadow Banking in China. In December 2012, 40 investors stood outside a Shanghai branch of the Huaxia (pronounced Wah Sha) Bank and protested. They had put their money in a wealth management product that had defaulted. Gong, a retired worker, said she was convinced by Pu Tingting, a customer manager at the Huaxia branch in a Shanghai suburb, to buy the product. "She told me the branch's chief had also bought the product," Gong said. "I trusted the bank and its staff, so I decided to buy, too." Investors stood to lose as much as 500 million renminbi (South China Morning Post 2012). Even worse, it looked like the bank had been raising money to pay off an earlier WMP that had defaulted, in a kind of illegal Ponzi scheme (Financial Times 2012). That episode didn't escalate into a full-blown crisis—but in future, it could.

The industry continues to grow. The outstanding value of WMPs rose to 23.5 trillion renminbi, or 35 percent of China's gross domestic product, at the end of 2015, from 7.1 trillion yuan three years earlier, according to China Central Depository and Clearing Co. An average of 3,500

WMPs were issued every week that year, with some smaller banks, such as China Merchants Bank Co. and China Everbright Bank Co., especially dependent on the products for funding. Interbank holdings of WMPs rose to 3 trillion renminbi at the end of 2015, from 496 billion yuan a year earlier. As much as 85 percent of those products may have been bought by other WMPs (Charlene 2016).

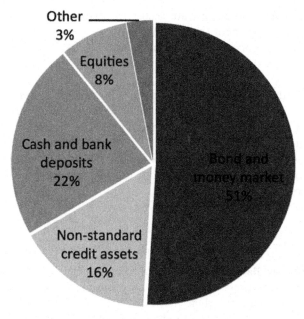

Fig. 11.1 Allocation of China's wealth management products by investment (2015) (*Source*: China Central Depository and Clearing Co.)

Not only is Shadow Banking growing rapidly but it is becoming more complex. Charlene Chu, a former Federal Reserve analyst now with an independent research firm in New York, argues that China is moving closer to a US-style risky "financialization" of its Shadow Banking sector.

When banks invest in each other's WMPs, this makes the pools of assets and liabilities tied to WMPs in effect second balance sheets, but with nothing but on-balance-sheet liquidity, reserves, and capital to meet payouts and absorb losses. These hidden balance sheets are beginning to undermine the integrity of banks' published balance sheets. "We're starting to see layers of liabilities built upon the same underlying assets, much like we did with subprime asset-backed securities, collateralized debt obligations, and CDOs-squared in the U.S.," Chu noted, (Bloomberg, May 30, 2016).

I witnessed this firsthand. In December 2013, traders around the world looked at their Bloomberg terminals and saw an alarming chart: interbank rates in China were skyrocketing. Rates that banks charge each other to lend money almost tripled from 4.5 percent to more than 10 percent. Traders scratched their heads trying to figure out how such a big move could happen—and why. They were worried this sudden rate rise signaled a financial crisis.

The rate hikes suddenly aimed a spotlight on an important area of Chinese banking—interbank borrowing. It turned out that it was not a full-blown crisis; instead, the PBOC was just trying to scare the banks by withdrawing liquidity from the market. It certainly did that. One official with a bank in Beijing was struggling for short-term cash. "During the crisis, our chairman called his friends at ICBC, which is the largest bank and well connected to the PBOC, and the postal bank, and borrowed 3 billion renminbi from the Postal Bank and 1 billion renminbi from ICBC," the executive in charge of international loans said (Interview, Beijing Bank, 2013). While the formal loan- to-deposit ratio was 75 percent, the ratio of loans and interbank assets to deposits rose to around 120 percent in 2013 and 2014 (Wright 2014). This type of financial episode could escalate in future.

However, despite the rapid growth of WMPs, and of interbank borrowing, since 2013 a crisis hasn't happened. Why not? The reasons are likely as follows:

1) Investors have implicit faith that the government will support almost all financial products, particularly those sold by banks (moral hazard).
2) Banks are devising new products that expand their balance sheets and help to prop up the industry.
3) Beijing is providing additional capital to support key corporates, thus averting default in their bonds (in which many WMPs invest) or their Shadow Banking instruments.
4) Local governments have discovered clever ways to raise capital through additional land sales or by convincing banks to roll over loans.

But what happens if these tricks no longer work?

The worst case for Shadow Banking would be a complete collapse in confidence in the entire industry. A rapid rise in default of Shadow Banking products, such as WMPs, would cause a crisis among private lenders. Shadow loans would dry up. Since approximately 40 percent of outstanding credit is from the Shadow Banks, this would have an instant impact on many institutions, both private and state-owned. Also, as noted above, many WMPs are increasingly invested between banks, raising the prospect of systemic risk to the economy. Small businesses—fledgling capitalism—would be hardest hit due to their reliance on Shadow Loans.

However, in our view, the worst case scenario is unlikely to occur. One reason is due to the highly interactive nature of China's political system. Political scientist Susan Shirk calls this "reciprocal accountability." She describes it thusly:

> Unlike a democracy, in which the people are sovereign, or an absolute monarchy or dictatorship, reciprocal accountability is a relationship in which neither side has a definitive right. The lines of authority run in both directions. (Ibid., *The Political Logic of Economic Reform.* Location 884)

The State Council becomes aware about local protests or incidents of severe financial pressure through a variety of channels, most often through the provincial officials with whom they are allied. Therefore, our supposition is that the State Council, or one of the leading working groups within the Politburo, would put pressure on banks to provide capital to prevent local unrest from escalating into a political crisis. However, that doesn't eliminate the prospect of a financial crisis, a crisis that overwhelms the capacity of the banks to respond. What would happen then?

* * *

Our "crystal gazing" envisions a future where China essentially runs out of capital to support everyone in the system. Defaulting Shadow Loans, along with formal credit, could swamp the banks.

The history of Shadow Banking in China tells us that capital flows outside of the formal state structure have been permitted and have grown. Apart from the shutdown of rural cooperatives in the 1990s by Premier Zhu Rongji, who was concerned about a rash of financial defaults, Shadow Banking's rise has been inexorable.

Shadow Banking has carved out an important place in Chinese economic life. It has performed two valuable functions. One, it has operated as a kind of a "fiscal glue," an implicit source of capital from the private sector for public ends. And two, it has been an escape valve for free-market activity in ways that do not overtly threaten the viability of the Communist Party or the state-controlled system. This escape valve works both for savers and for users of capital. We believe these functions will continue, and are likely to grow over time.

However, China is currently facing the very difficult problems of high debt levels and a slowing economy. These issues will constrain the growth of credit, forcing increasingly difficult decisions about who is funded by the state. Non-state sources of credit from Shadow Banks will be more difficult to obtain as defaults increase, scaring investors from providing additional funds. The state will become more selective about which institutions will be granted bank loans. In addition, the political centralization mandated by President Xi Jinping will constrain the state's choices in allocating capital.

The "deleveraging" will result in a difficult transition as Beijing struggles between the poles of paying down debt and maintaining growth. As former World Bank economist Yukon Huang noted, "The process, however, will be messy and costly as the economy slowly hemorrhages financial resources in supporting these bailouts and is forced to throw good money after bad to keep growth in line with official targets" (Huang and Bosler 2014).

This is where our analysis becomes highly speculative. Any prognosis for the future of China should be taken with a grain of salt. However, we'll give it a try.

We see China splitting into two camps as a result of these economic forces. The first camp will consist of Beijing and a few top cities such as Shanghai and Guangzhou. They will protect their favored state firms, elites who are involved in them, and the most important banks. Alongside these will be a host of protected state firms in other regions that have tight political links with either Beijing officials or members of the State Council. In addition, state firms with large numbers of employees that are easily mobilized into potential protesting groups will be granted sufficient capital to financial problems that could lead to massive unrest.

The opposing camp will not be a member of this charmed circle. This group would include the more impoverished smaller cities and remoter provinces, whose state firms wield insufficient political power to marshal resources from the political center in Beijing. Independent macroeconomic research firm Gavekal identifies three criteria for companies that will suffer defaults: those experiencing financial stress, those in excess capacity sectors, and those small enough to lack friends in high places. The latter criterion will be crucial (Gatley and Long 2014).

This process we call the *"Tightening Circle of Capital."* Capital will flow to the powerful sectors and withdraw from the weaker ones—except on those occasions when social unrest forces the leadership to spread capital over a wider group of actors. The capital also will drift to large SOEs, which tend to generate lower returns.

What we will see over time is a gradual narrowing of the circle of capital. Weaker provinces, smaller state firms, and SMEs will be squeezed out of the circle, leaving only the larger SOEs and cities including Beijing, Shanghai, and Guangzhou with priority access to capital. Some data currently supports this admittedly speculative hypothesis. One-third of 122.8 trillion renminbi of aggregate financing in 2014 (including most Shadow Loans) went to just three places: Beijing and the provinces containing the large cities of Guangzhou and Shanghai. One could argue a similar concentration of wealth is occurring elsewhere in the globe. In the USA, the per capita income of Washington, D.C., in 1980 was 29 percent above the average for Americans as a whole; in 2013, that figure was 68 percent. In San Francisco, per capita income jumped from 50 percent to 88 percent above average over that period; in New York, from 80 percent to 172 percent (Macgillis 2016).

In China, we believe this concentration of wealth will accelerate, resulting in several outcomes:

First, regional credit institutions will be allowed to fail. In Japan in 1994, the Tokyo Government closed the Tokyo Kyowa Credit Cooperative and Anzen Credit Cooperative, followed in 1995, by the Cosmo Credit Cooperative (Tokyo) and the Kizu Credit Cooperative (Osaka). Larger financial institutions fell later. China has done this in the past in 1999 with the closure of 18,000 Rural Credit Foundations.

Second, weak local SOEs will be shuttered or be absorbed by larger SOEs. The lucky ones will be acquired depending on their political clout and size of employment.

Third, SOE banks will find their margins shrinking. This will occur in several ways: through programs like the local bond swap that lowered returns, the debt for equity that eliminates debt payments, and other bail-out programs.

Fourth, debt will be centralized—but not in obvious ways. Expanding central government bonds is anathema to the leadership as the leadership appears adamant on maintaining a low ratio of central government debt to GDP. Instead, the various forms of corporate and local debt will be monetized through stealth programs like the local bond swap.

Fifth, SMEs in many areas of the country will resort to high-interest Shadow Loans that will be increasingly difficult to obtain.

This is a decidedly speculative prediction of the future of Shadow Banking and the Chinese economy. But recent events support this theory.

***

We are already starting to see struggles for dwindling capital. In September 2016, at the time of writing, Dongbei Special Steel, a leading producer of special alloys for automobiles, defaulted on the repayment of seven bonds with a combined value of 3.1 billion renminbi. The State-owned Assets Supervision and Administration Commission (SASAC) of the Liaoning Provincial Government, which held 46 percent of the company's shares and was the largest shareholder, drafted a plan to resolve the company's debt problems.

In a surprising show of strength, the bondholders not only protested the plan—but asked investors nationwide to boycott bonds issued by any companies in Liaoning province. The bondholders and the banks both were protesting because the plan called for banks to swap 70 percent of their loans to the steel company into equity, and for the lead underwriters of the bonds to lend the firm money to allow it to repay the remainder of the outstanding bonds. Essentially, the banks and the bondholders would be stuck with the bad debt, instead of the Liaoning government.

"Banks were shut out of all meetings the government held to discuss how to resolve the problem, even though they are the largest creditors," according to an executive with one of the company's creditor banks. "The plan is all about protecting the government's own interest as much as possible, with no consideration at all given to the lawful interests of other bond holders," a bond investor said. "It is not feasible at all" (Investors Seek Liaoning Debt Boycott As Bond Default Battle Heats Up. *Caixin Magazine*, July 19, 2016).

Who was responsible for the debt? Debt holders included state banks, private banks, and private investors through the bond market. Although it was not stated, the debt likely included Shadow Banking loans through the Trusts or the WMPs. Would the Liaoning government choose to: a) close Dongbei Steel, b) agree to the bondholder demands and find money to repay them, or c) use political connections to receive a bailout from Beijing?

The latter solution was quite likely. The banks may have had to accept the loss in this case because the Liaoning government is quite well connected. Liaoning's party secretary, Li Xi, knew President Xi Jinping in Shaanxi province, where President Xi had spent seven years during the Cultural Revolution.

This was a brawl between competing financial and governmental groups, including private investors in public bonds and Shadow debt, local governments, and the banks. This is just one example among many that will play out across China.

*　*　*

Decisions about who will and who will not be part of the "Tightening Circle of Capital" will be determined by the institutions that have the most control. Providing a detailed map of power relations in China is a large topic beyond the scope of this book. There are many competing theories about how to analyze power relations in China. But we can make a few generalizations.

One of the key conflicts will be between the institutions that control the economy in Beijing. These include the Ministry of Finance, the PBOC, and the CBRC. They have differing agendas. As political scientist Susan Shirk notes: "Ministry of Finance officials are always worried revenues will not grow to cover their increasing expenses. Financial officials are 'savers' whereas officials in industrial ministries and provincial governments generally are 'spenders.'" Ibid, Shirk, Susan. *The Political Logic of Economic Reform*, Location 1013. The spenders generally are in the State Council and in the provincial and lower levels of government. They depend on fiscal revenue for growth and career advancement. The savers are allied with the Ministry of Finance, the People's Bank of China, and the China Banking Regulatory Commission. Their careers rely on preventing inflation, halting asset bubbles, and ensuring adequate governmental revenue.

Within the bureaucracy, the People's Bank of China is a well-respected institution, and its success over the previous two decades has given it a degree of independence from the State Council. In contrast, the National Development and Reform Commission (NDRC), the former state planning board, functions as an advisor to the State Council on economic matters. But that means it also is subject to the various factions within the Council. Also, as the former planning board, it is much more interested in spending than saving money.

In addition, of course, the personal views of President Xi or a subsequent leader will be crucial in determining the outcome of this forced restructuring. President Xi is clearly in favor of strong state firms. He has said state firms must have "a dominant role in important sectors and crucial areas that affect national security and the commanding heights of the economy" (Naughton 2016).

In addition, as capital becomes more scarce, the relationship between the provinces and the central government in Beijing will play an important role. This includes the formal fiscal relationship, in terms of which government pays for which social services that we discussed in the section on Federalism. It also will include the informal linkages between provincial officials and Beijing. For example, at the time of writing, there were five State Council officials who presided over province or province-level cities. These were Han Zheng in Shanghai, Hu Chunhua in Guangdong, Sun Zhengcai in Chongqing, Zhang Chunxian in Xinjiang, and Guo Jinlong in Beijing. They are likely to defend their local interests, including local SOEs.

As political economist Victor Shih noted: "Factions led by senior party functionaries mainly comprise provincial officials and have the strongest control over the party apparatus....on the other hand, there are factions led by senior officials with narrower experience in the regime. They often rise vertically within a certain bureaucratic group" (Shih, Victor. *Finance and Factions in China*. Location 238).

There are many links between the provinces and Beijing. From personal experience, I have witnessed this during trips to China with investors. At one private gathering in a hotel in Xian to discuss China's growing debt, we met with Bank of China executives, and officials from the local government and other agencies, including the PBOC and the

CBRC. As the conference ended, I privately asked my Bank of China colleague how the local debt burden would be handled. "We meet to discuss that every week," she said. The PBOC and the CBRC were receiving orders from Beijing. Meanwhile, the local government officials had their own agenda. The Bank of China executive—whose bank held much of the debt—was caught in the middle between her bosses in Beijing, the regulators, and the local officials. This local discussion was a good example of Shirk's "reciprocal accountability" between Beijing and the provinces.

As China confronts the debt created by the formal and Shadow Banking economy, we can expect that there will be a tug-of-war among institutions in China about who is going to get stuck with the debt—and how much would be Beijing's responsibility. The USA went through the same process during the mortgage crisis. Former US Treasury Secretary Timothy Geithner struggled with many of the issues that China is likely to confront in the near future. As he noted about the banks during the US crisis:

> There was a widespread belief, often tinged with moral fervor, that we needed to cleanse their balance sheets of toxic junk, to "scrub their books" so they could lend again....Nobody had good answers to the problems of how we would decide which assets to buy or guarantee, how much to pay for them, and how to avoid getting taken to the cleaners by the banks that knew the details of their assets much better than we did. (Geithner 2014b)

Throughout this book we have emphasized the tremendous differences in political, economic, and financial control between Beijing and the provinces, and even between provinces. These risks are likely to be exacerbated as China's slowing GDP takes hold and credit dries up. We can see the regional disparities particularly sharply if we look at the Shadow Banking exposure between provinces.

Nicholas Borst, a former analyst at the Peterson Institute in Washington and now at the Federal Reserve in San Francisco, analyzed the regional breakdown of Shadow Banking assets using data from the central bank. There are significant regional differences. The top ten areas exposed to Shadow Banking in 2013 according to share of Total Social Financing ranged from Shanghai (46 percent) to Hebei (38 percent).

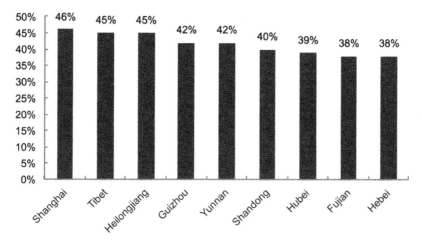

Fig. 11.2 Top ten areas in China exposed to Shadow Banking (% TSF) (*Source*: Peterson Institute)

He concludes:

> The provinces with higher levels of exposure these off-balance sheet products will be more vulnerable to defaults and financial distress as these products mature. A natural response for financial regulators in these areas would be to apply heightened scrutiny to local financial institutions. (Borst 2014)

The problems from regional exposure to Shadow Banking products will be further stressed by weak local economies. Local governments with ailing industries are likely to have chased after Shadow Products as a source of capital to fund infrastructure or to pump air into property.

To go back to the argument about the Tightening Circle of Capital, areas with larger exposure to Shadow Banking are likely to have weaker links to Beijing; after all, they're getting less money from the banks, and more from private sources. Therefore, they will be less able to commandeer resources from Beijing during a period of trouble.

***

There are some indicators from China's recent history how China will "cleanse the balance sheets" of the banks, as Geithner put it. Several relatively new economic actors have sprung up that have become power-ful political actors. Among these are Huarong Asset Management and its three other sister asset management companies (AMCs).

The Chinese central AMCs arguably are going to be among the key institutions in disposing of bad loans in the coming decades as Beijing struggles with defaults caused by lower GDP growth. The irony is that these AMCs were specifically designed to have a short shelf life. The four of them—Huarong, Great Wall, Orient, and Cinda—were originally set up to go out of business by the early part of the twenty-first century. They were created in the late 1990s for a specific purpose—to take on the bad debt of the four state banks so the banks could be profitable enough to list on the stock exchange. After that, they were scheduled to fade away.

However, they had several advantages that kept them in business. First, during the initial listing of the banks, the AMCs obtained loans at favor-able rates from the Ministry of Finance. Second, the property boom made their assets, much of them in the form of commercial and residential prop-erty, more valuable over time. Last, as with most bureaucracies, they man-aged to carve out new niches for themselves by obtaining licenses to enter new areas, such as stock and bond trading and other aspects of the securi-ties business. So when Xi and his colleagues were looking for an institu-tion to step in quickly, and quietly, and resolve difficult situations such as Zhenfu's embarrassing 3 billion renminbi bad debt, Huarong AMC was an ideal fit. The money, as usual, came from the state banks, and in the case of Zhenfu, this was ICBC.

These days, we can think of the AMCs as the "gunslingers" of modern Chinese finance; like the sheriffs of the American Wild West, they will ride in and clean up the town—getting rid not of outlaws but of bad debt. Why would they be appointed town sheriff?

The AMCS are headquartered in Beijing and thus are more closely con-nected to the State Council than organizations elsewhere in the country. They have a wide mandate, which they are expanding, and are available for all sorts of financial troubleshooting. In fact, Beijing has ordered the creation of more than a dozen local AMCs in the provinces to perform much the same job: swoop in to handle bad debt. There is some debate about how effective these "mini-AMCs" will be given their lack of capital and modest access to the coffers of the state banking system. There is some speculation that eventually these mini-AMCs will simply be acquired by the Beijing AMCs and become their local arms. In that case, we would be looking at a system where local debt would become the property of the state banking system.

Someone will have to take a loss on the loans sold by the AMCs. That will entail significant discounts and will depend on negotiations—loan by loan. For example, in 2013, one 1.8 billion renminbi Bank of China was sold to an AMC for just 360 million renminbi—an 80 percent discount. The bank took the loss (Author's Interview, Bank of China, 2013).

But will these giant AMCs sweep in to dispose of *private debt* from the Shadow economy? After all, a large portion of Shadow Loans have come from private investors. The answer is—maybe. After all, the local bond swap in the provinces appears to include debt from private sources through Shadow Banking. Beijing will draw a line in the sand not based so much on whether the assets are private or state owned—but who is the most powerful. Therefore, a well-connected group of wealthy private investors in the tony suburbs of Beijing could be repaid on a bad loan ahead of an ailing state steel company in a distant province. That is the "Tightening Circle of Capital" at work.

***

Will China's downturn halt the flow of capital to small, private businesses, preventing capitalism from flourishing?

Political economist Yukong Huang believes Shadow Banking has fueled the expansion of the state.

"The image of a powerful state sector comes out most vividly in the role that land development has played in driving economic expansion in recent years. Much of this development was accomplished by local authorities through their links with LGFVs. By tapping their access to state-controlled land, authorities were able to finance a range of investments even if many of the actual developers were private entities. That much of this activity *was being financed by Shadow Banking* involving complex arrangements between private and state-owned financial entities exaggerated the sense that the state was somehow manipulating things." (Book Review, *Markets over Mao*, p. 147, Asia Policy, Number 20, July 2015, p. 153).

Others agree that LGFVs worked hand-in-hand with Shadow Banks for state ends. For example, before 2008, the China Development Bank was the primary source for local government financing. In November 2008, commercial banks started to aggressively lend to local governments. These were usually short-term loans of one to three years. In 2010, the central government decided to slow the stimulus. As a result, many commercial banks either stopped lending or rolled loans over to local governments. "However, local governments' investments are usually long-term (such as infrastructure investments), and they needed loans to continue projects begun under the stimulus program. Therefore, after 2010, many local governments started issuing bonds and *borrowing from shadow banking systems* in China" (Ru 2015, p. 11).

However, the LGFVs are only one recipient of Shadow Banking loans. As we have seen, much of the credit was absorbed by private entrepreneurs. Even now, there is the potential for new growth among small firms. And this is where Shadow Banking is likely to play a crucial role by allocating capital to the more productive SMEs.

Kellee Tsai of HKUST speaks of a "parallel political economy" that resulted from the explosion of Shadow Banking in the past decade. This parallel economy is essentially a private channel of capital flows from lenders to borrowers that has expanded far beyond what the government anticipated when it unleashed the stimulus package.

> Indeed, the scope of informal finance has expanded into the broader universe of shadow banking, which involves not just private entrepreneurs, but middle-class professionals seeking wealth management products and local governments facing unfunded mandates and incentives to demonstrate economic development. Arguably, the contemporary map of informal finance and shadow banking represents a parallel political economy that complements, and is therefore just as functionally entrenched as, the vested interests in the state sector. (Tsai 2015a)

Shadow Banking now combines local government bureaucrats and party members, dynamic entrepreneurs, shysters and boiler-room financiers, and reaches all the way to the headquarters of the giant state banks in Beijing, which jumped eagerly into Shadow Banking once they witnessed the profits they could reap.

It will be difficult for Beijing to shut down this parallel political economy. The middle class likes the new investment options, local governments need this private source of revenue, and banks have fattened their profits by selling new financial products. Beijing can't put the Shadow Banking genie back in the bottle.

But what about capitalist enterprises? Will the parallel economy include them, at a time when growth is slowing and money is tight? The answer is yes—but this may occur in unexpected ways.

In a fascinating paper, Harvard Business School Assistant Professor Meg Rithmire examined city competition in two northern Chinese cities, Dalian and Harbin. Dalian is a port city that in 1984 was designated one of 14 ports with special trade privileges. In the late 1990s, the strong-willed Bo Xilai relocated 115 enterprises out of the downtown area, freeing up land for city use. Bo's political power, early push for investment funds, and favorable Beijing policies allowed Dalian to grab domestic and foreign capital early. The city did well—using classic state strategies. Other cities tried to follow Dalian's lead but lost out because Dalian had an "early mover" advantage; the low-hanging fruit of mobile capital was gone.

Rithmire contrasted Dalian's experience with Harbin. As an inland city in China's industrial northeast, faced with outdated industries, Harbin lacked access to capital, and had to struggle on its own. The city found a way through entrepreneurship. "Harbin, like other regional cities without extensive access to foreign capital and investment, attempted to grow through streamlining the public economy and nurturing small-scale entrepreneurship. The municipal government was challenged to execute politically difficult enterprise reforms in a climate of scarcity and fear of social instability," Rithmire noted. Due to the strength of local state firms and the weakness of the city government—along with a shortage of new capital—Harbin struggled, but eventually succeeded in moving forward (Rithmire 2013).

Rithmire praised the state-controlled industrialized Harbin for *moving faster into capitalism*—or at least small-scale free markets—than the slick Dalian. "By 1981, the city had registered over 12,000 private enterprises, 21 times the number registered at the end of 1978. Critically, the onus of encouraging, registering and approving private enterprise rested with lower levels of government. The blossoming of commercial activity—shoe repair, craftsmanship, barber shops, food stalls, teahouses, bakeries and the like—emerged under the purview of street offices" (Rithmire, Ibid, p. 18). She doesn't detail the source capital for these small businesses, but one can assume much of it came from informal finance—family, local cooperatives, or other businesses. In other words, Shadow Banking. Amidst the hulk of the dilapidated state firms, capitalism flourished as the state retreated. And Shadow Banking played an important role.

The parable here for the rest of China is that cities with political clout, and which jump in early to become the leader in a certain industry, can do well. But most will not. Imitators fall by the wayside, deluding themselves that building yet another "Economic Development Zone" would solve their fiscal problems. All this shell game does is consume loans (both bank and Shadow Bank) that support property prices, giving the illusion of economic success, without the reality of real economic activity.

Thus, we end the book on a hopeful note. The Tightening Circle of Capital may have benefits. Local governments, squeezed for revenue, will reduce support for state firms. Beijing will turn a blind eye to many struggling localities as they hoard their remaining financial resources. Meanwhile, entrepreneurs, encouraged by desperate local officials, will launch small businesses amidst the looming hulks of dilapidated state firms, like hardy dandelions growing in a garbage dump. Only time will tell whether this scenario will come true. More important, only time will tell how the leaders in Beijing handle this economic revolution, seeded by Shadow Banking.

Bibliography

Admati, A., & Hellwig, M. (2013). *The bankers' new clothes* (p. 61). Princeton: Princeton University Press.

Allen, F., Qian, J., & Qian, M. (2009). China's financial system. In L. Brandt & T. Rawski (Eds.), *China's great economic transformation*. Cambridge: Cambridge University Press. Kindle edition, location 11775.

Anderson, J. (2014, October 17). Emerging advisors group. *Real Economics vs. China Economics.*

Ayyagari, M., Demirguc-Kunt, A., & Maksimovic, V. (2007, March). *Formal versus informal finance: Evidence from China*. Washington, DC: World Bank.

Bank of China. (2013). Author Interview.

Bank of Jinzhou, IPO Prospectus.

Bank of Tianjin Listing Prospectus, p. 31.

Bedford, J. (2016, June 2). *Shadow loan books, WMPs and a Rmb1trn capital hole*. Hong Kong: UBS.

Bing, Z. (2014, January 22). Yu E Bao deals with the pressure of being no. 1. *Caixin.*

Bloomberg News. *Death and despair in China's rustbelt*, March 1, 2016.

Borst, N. (2013, August). *Measuring excess credit growth*. Washington, DC: Peterson Institute.

Borst, N. (2014, February 21). *A map of china's shadow banking exposure*. Washington, DC: Peterson Institute.

Bottelier, P. (2015, June). *Shadow banking in China*. Washington, DC: World Bank.

Caixin, *Investors in troubled trust product told they'll be repaid*, January 28, 2014.

Caixin, *Regulators ready to Defog P2P lending sector*, December 10, 2015.

Caixin Magazine, *Sisters in the shadows of a Shanxi graft probe*, May 14, 2014.

© The Author(s) 2017
A. Collier, *Shadow Banking and the Rise of Capitalism in China*,
DOI 10.1007/978-981-10-2996-7

Calomiris, C. W., & Haber, S. H. (2014). *Fragile by design: The political origins of banking crises & scarce credit* (p. 13). Princeton: Princeton University Press.

Charlene Chu, Autonomous Research, cited in Bloomberg. *China default chain reaction threatens products worth 35% of GDP*, May 30, 2016.

Chen, K., et al. (2016). *What we learn from China's rising shadow banking: Exploring the Nexus of monetary tightening and banks' role in entrusted lending.* NBER. http://www.nber.org/papers/w21890

China.org.cn. November 10, 2008.

China Vast Industrial Corp., Offering Prospectus, Hong Kong. August 13, 2014.

Chivakul, M., et al. (2015). *Understanding residential real estate in China.* Washington, DC: IMF. Financial distortions in China: A general equilibrium approach. Prepared by Diego Anzoategui, Mali Chivakul, and Wojciech Maliszewski. Authorized for distribution by James Daniel December 2015.

Citic. www.citic.com/AboutUs/History

Dang, T. V., Wang, H., & Yao, A. (2015a, December). *Chinese shadow banking: Bank-centric misperceptions.* Hong Kong: Hong Kong Institute for Monetary Research.

Dang, T. V., Wang, H., & Yao, A. (2015b, December). *Shadow banking modes: The Chinese versus the U.S. system* (Working paper). New York: Columbia University.

Das, U. S., Fiechter, J., & Sun, T. (2013). China's road to greater financial stability: Some policy perspectives. In Y. Li and X. Zhang (Eds.), *China's sovereign balance sheet.* Washington, DC: International Monetary Fund.

Deer, L. (2013). *Entrusted lending.* Frontiers of Finance in China, blog, Sydney.

East Asia Forum. (2010, January 24). Accessed at http://www.eastasiaforum. org/2010/01/24/chinas-response-to-the-global-financial-crisis/

Economist. Collapse of Gitic, January 14, 1999.

Elliott, D., Kroeber, A., & Qiao, Y. (2015). *Shadow banking in China: A primer.* Washington, DC: Brookings Institution.

Fabre, G. (2013). *What's behind China's slowdown* (Working paper). Fondation Maison des Science de L'homme.

Financial Stability Board, Basel, Switzerland. (2015a). *Shadow banking monitoring report.* Basel: Financial Stability Board.

Financial Stability Board, Basle, Switzerland. (2015b). *Global shadow banking monitoring report 2015* (p. 44). Basel: Financial Stability Board.

Financial Times. *China's banking Weapons of Mass Ponzi problem pops up again.* December 11, 2012.

Finder, S. (2015, June 5). Shadow banking cases threaten to overwhelm China's courts. *The Diplomat.*

Finder, S. (2016, March). *Supreme People's Court Monitor*, Hong Kong. https:// supremepeoplescourtmonitor.com/2016/03/

FT story. (2016, May). China financial regulator.

Gang, X. *Regulating shadow banking.* http://www.chinadaily.com.cn/opinion/2012-10/12/content_15812305.htm

Gao, H., Ru, H., & Tang, D. Y. (2016). *Subnational debt: The politics finance Nexus*. Unpublished Paper, University of Hong Kong.

Gatley, T., & Long, C. (2014, April). Defaults are coming—Where, when and how. *Gavekal Dragonomics*.

Geithner, T. (2014a). *Stress test*. New York: Crown Publishing.

Geithner, T. (2014b). *Stress test: Reflections on financial crises*. New York: Crown Publishing Group.

Global Stability Report. IMF, 2015, p. 17.

Hong Kong Institute for Monetary Research, December 2015.

Hu, F. (2015, August 28). *China's financial future: Shadow banking in China*. Panel discussion, Asia Global Institute, University of Hong Kong, Hong Kong.

Huang, Y., & Bosler, C. (2014, September). *China's debt dilemma*. Washington, DC: Carnegie Endowment.

Huang, Y., & Wang, X. (2010). *Does financial repression inhibit economic growth*. China Center for Economic Research, Peking University, China.

International Monetary Fund (IMF). (2013, October). *Local government financing platforms in China: A fortune or misfortune* (p. 11). Washington, DC: IMF.

International Monetary Fund (IMF). (2014, January). *Fiscal vulnerabilities and risks from local government finance* (p. 7). Washington, DC: International Monetary Fund.

Investors seek Liaoning Debt Boycott as bond default battle heats up. (2016, July 19). *Caixin Magazine*.

Kissinger, H. (2011). *On China*. London: Penguin Press.

Kumar, A., Lardy, N., Albrecht, W., Chuppe, T., Selwyn, S., Perttunen, P., & Zhang, T. (1997). *China's non-bank financial institutions: Trust and investment companies* (World Bank Discussion Papers; no. WDP 358). Washington, DC: The World Bank.

Lardy, N. (2008, September). *Financial repression in China*. Washington, DC: Peterson Institute.

Lardy, N. (2012). *Sustaining China's economic growth after the great financial crisis*. Location 1883. Washington, DC: Peterson Institute.

Lardy, N. *Markets over Mao*. Location 2626.

Lei, K. (2016, May 4). *Closing loophole on improper NPLs disposal is positive in long run*. Hong Kong: J.P. Morgan Research.

Li, J., & Hsu, S. (2009). *Informal finance in China. Chapter on the evolution of informal finance*. Oxford: Oxford Scholarship.

Li, J., & Hsu, S. (2013). *Shadow banking in China: Institutional risks*. Amherst: University of Massachusetts.

Li, J., & Hsu, S. (2014). *Shadow banking and systemic risk in China* (p. 15). Amherst: University of Massachusetts.

Liao, M., Sun, T., & Zhang, J. (2016, August). *China's financial linkages and implications for inter-agency cooperation* (Working paper). Washington, DC: IMF.

Liu, Y.-L. (1992). Reform from below: *The private economy and local politics in the rural industrialization of Wenzhou. China Quarterly, 130,* 293–298.

Lu, Y, & Sun, T. (2013). *Local government financing platforms in China: A fortune or misfortune?* (IMF working paper). Washington, DC: International Monetary Fund.

Macgillis, A. (2016, September). The original underclass. *The Atlantic.*

Mehrling, P. (2016, June 2). *Learning to think about shadow banking,* Blog.

Ministry of Finance, Local Fiscal Statistical Yearbook, 2011.

Naughton, B. (2016, Summer). *Two trains running: Supply-side reform, SOE reform and the authoritative personage* (China Leadership Monitor, No. 50). Stanford: Hoover Institution.

Ong, L. (2012). *Prosper or perish: Credit and fiscal systems in early China.* Ithaca: Cornell University Press.

Orient Capital Research, Hong Kong. Interview, 2015.

Pantsov, A., & Levine, S. (2015). *Deng Xiaoping, a revolutionary life* (p. 372). Oxford: Oxford University Press.

Perry, E., & Weltewitz, F. (2015, June). Wealth management products in China. Sydney. *Bulletin.*

Pettis, M. (2013). *Avoiding the fall: China's economic restructuring* (p. 133). Washington, DC: Carnegie Endowment for International Peace.

Powell, B. (2010, November 17). Chanos versus China. *Fortune.*

Pozsar, Z., et al. (2010). *Federal Reserve Bank of New York Staff Report* (Staff Report No. 458). Revised February 2012.

Qizheng, M. (2013, February). *Measuring the off-balance-sheet wealth management business of commercial banks—The case in China* (International Finance Corporation Bulletin No. 36). Washington, DC: International Finance Corporation.

Reuters. (2014, March 6). *Rural mini-bank run highlights perils of deregulation in China.* London: Reuters.

Reuters. (2016, February 1). *China arrests Ezubo-linked suspects over $7.6 billion Ponzi Scheme.* London: Reuters.

Rithmire, M. (2013, November). Land politics and local state capacities: The political economy of urban change in China. *China Quarterly,* p. 9.

Ru, H. (2015). *Government credit, a double-edged Sword: Evidence from the China development bank* (p. 70). Aldan, PA: Hong Ru, MIT.

Rural Bank of Beijing, Author's Interview, March 5, 2016.

Shen, W. (2012). Shadow banking system in China—Origin, uniqueness and governmental responses. *Annals of Economics and Finance, 13*(1), 1–51.

Shen, C., Jin, J., & Zou, H. F. (2012a). Fiscal decentralization in China: History, impact, challenges and next steps. *Annals of Economics and Finance, 13*(1), 1–51.

Shen, C., Jin, J., & Zou, H.-f. (2012b). *Fiscal decentralization in China.* Beijing: Central University of Finance and Economics.

Shih, V. (2008). *Factions and finance in China*. Cambridge: Cambridge University Press, Introduction.

Shih, V., Zhang, Q., & Liu, M. (2008). *When the autocrat gives: Determinants of fiscal transfers in China*. Victor Shih, Department of Political Science, Northwestern University, unpublished paper.

Shih, V., et al. (2012, February). Getting ahead in the communist party: Explaining the advancement of central committee members in China. *American Political Science Review, 106*(1). doi:10.1017/S0003055411000566.

Shirk, S. (1993). *The political logic of economic reform in China*. Berkeley: University of California Press.

Shougang Fushan Financial Filing, 2013.

Solow, R. (2013, April 8). How to save American finance from itself. *New Republic*.

South China Morning Post, *Huaxia scandal spotlights China's Ponzi crisis*. December 10, 2012.

South China Morning Post, *Risky business of P2P lending*. January 16, 2016a

South China Morning Post, *Unrest risk from internet financial fraud rise*. January 16, 2016b

Stevenson-Yang, A. (2015, March 30). Why near term financial crisis looms. *J Capital Research*.

Tam, O.-K. (1986). Reform of China's banking system. *World Economy, 9*(4), 427–440.

Tanaka, K., & Monar, M. (2008). What is different about informal finance. *Revue Economique, 59*, 1131–1143. Sciences Po: Paris.

Tao, W. (2014, March 27). *Business Insider Magazine*.

Taplin, N. (2015, March 16). *In China, trust firms shift, rather than reduce, shadow banking risk*. London: Reuters.

Tsai, K. (2015a, March). *The political economy of state capitalism and shadow banking* (Issues and Studies, Vol. 51, pp. 55–97). Taipei: Institute of International Studies.

Tsai, K. (2015b). *The political economy of shadow banking* (HKUST Paper). Presentation to the Shadow Banking and Alternative Finance in China, Conference at the China Studies Centre at the University of Sydney, May 2016. Unpublished Paper.

Tsai, K. (2015c, June 5). *Keynote presentation at CUFE online finance conference*.

Tsai, K. (2016, May 27). *Presentation, workshop on "Shadow banking and alternative finance in China,"* China Studies Centre, University of Sydney.

Wildau, G. (2016, May 2). China financial regulator clamps down on shadow banking. *Financial Times*.

Wong, C. (2011). University of Oxford. Presentation to Investment Conference in Brasil.

Wong, C. (2013). Challenges of municipal finance. In R. W. Bahl, J. F. Linn, & D. L. Wetzel (Eds.), *Financing metropolitan governments in developing countries* (p. 6). Cambridge, MA: Lincoln Institute of Land Policy.

Wright, L. (2014). *Deliquification and China's deflationary adjustment.* New York: Medley Global Advisors.

Wu, W. (2016, January 16). Risky business of P2P lending. *South China Morning Post.*

Xinhua. (2008, November 9). *China's 4 trillion yuan stimulus to boost economy.* Accessed at http://news.xinhuanet.com/english/2008-11/09/content_10331324.htm

Xueqing, J. (2014, August 14). Trust companies get new guidelines from CBRC. *China Daily.*

Yang, J. (2016a, August 31). China P2P industry 'basically' a scam, Billionaire Guo says. *Bloomberg News.*

Yang, Y. (2016b, February 7). What stock market turmoil means for China's economy. *Financial Times.*

Yuan, T. (2014, October 24). *Rise and fall of a coal boomtown in Shanxi province.* Beijing: Caixin Magazine.

Zhang, Z. (2013, March 13). *China: Rising risks of financial crisis.* Hong Kong: Nomura Research.

Zhang, Y. S., & Barnett, S. (2014, January). *Fiscal vulnerabilities and risks from local government finance in China.* Washington, DC: IMF.

Zheng, L. (2015). *The shadow banking system of China and international regulatory cooperation.* Ontario: Centre for International Governance Regulation.

INDEX

© The Author(s) 2017
A. Collier, *Shadow Banking and the Rise of Capitalism in China*,
DOI 10.1007/978-981-10-2996-7

CPSIA information can be obtained
at www.ICGtesting.com
Printed in the USA
LVOW02*0415180517
534944LV00040B/1637/P